Chicken Caesar Salad

for the Gay Soul

Books by La'Von Gittens

The Divine Apocalypse Series
Divine Apocalypse: The Beginning of the End
Divine Apocalypse: Addiction and Clearing
Divine Apocalypse: Attis

Chicken Caesar Salad

for the Gay Soul

By La'Von Gittens

This book is a self help guide intended for educational purposes. Work included is public domain and or is donated by private sources. NoV'al Publishing does not own the rights to any educational studies, works of art, quotations, or citations.

Copyright © 2015

The information provided by NoV'al Publishing in the book *Chicken Caesar Salad For the Gay Soul* is for general informational and educational purposes only. All information in this book is provided in good faith, however we make no representation or warranty of any kind, express or implied, regarding the accuracy, adequacy, validity, reliability, availability or completeness of any information in this book. Under no circumstance shall we have any liability to you for any loss or damage of any kind incurred as a result of the use of the book or reliance on any information provided in this book *Chicken Caesar Salad For the Gay Soul*. Your use of the book and your reliance on any information in the book is solely at your own risk.

All rights reserved. No part of this book may be reproduced or used in any manner without written permission of the copyright owner except for the use of quotations in a book review.

First paperback published in 2015

Reprinted in 2021

ISBN: 9780984346646 (paperback)

Published by NoV'al Publishing

www.novalpublishing.com

To my mother and sisters who love and accept me for who I am

Table of Contents

Introduction

Chapter 1: What is Gay?

Chapter 2: Is it Natural?

Chapter 3: Gayness in History

Chapter 4: What Religion Has to Say

Chapter 5: Homophobia

Chapter 6: Mainstream Gayness

Chapter 7: Am I Gay?

Introduction

Why Should I Read this Book

Memories are our defining roots. All my life I've felt like an outsider, even in my own home. It took time. I never really understood my awkwardness; I just knew I was different.

Thanksgiving many years ago, I visited family that I rarely see. We laughed, ate, and reminisced. I had a great time until my uncle, who, as many uncles do, started into a twenty minute rant. In the same breath he told me that he loved me, he exclaimed several times over, "I HATE faggots!" The room fell completely silent. A wave of uneasiness washed over us. It felt like I was stripped naked and thrown onto center stage. I looked towards my mother and sisters as they turned away without words. I wiped away a guilty sweat, then lowered my head. My eyes welled up and my heart was in my throat. I was confused, and the shame followed me for years.

I am sorry that he and so many others feel that way. I hope to change their minds.

With the release of this book, I am coming out as a homosexual man to my family and the entire world. Until now, I have kept my personal relationships a secret because of the deep rooted shame embedded in me by a homophobic society. I love and respect all of you, but this is what I must do.

Family and friends, I know that some are confused, angry, or even embarrassed that I chose this platform to reveal myself; however, with the growing rate of homosexual suicides, I can no longer keep silent.

This book is filled with empowering truths. I keep these facts close to my heart. Knowledge has saved my life, and I believe that it could do the same for others.

Suicide has proven to be an unfortunate alternative for homosexual youth, more so than for heterosexual youth. In my lifetime, I have seen death, and it has broken my heart. According to The Trevor Project, LGB youth are five times more likely to attempt suicide than heterosexual youths, and 40% of transgender youth have attempted suicide. These are all losses that can be prevented.

Something needs to be done.

Every suicide represents a failure from society. These pages will satisfy a variety of readers including: straight men and women who have a desire to be well-informed or questioning individuals; parents of homosexual children; and, of course, my LGBTQ family. *Chicken Caesar Salad for the Gay Soul* serves as a factual portrayal of homosexuality that is not often seen in mainstream media and which may otherwise be unknown to the general public. Built within these pages is an informative guide throughout homosexual history and the beginning to a deeper understanding of our culture.

Chapter 1

What is Gay?

"To gay or not to gay, that is the question! I'm Leo the Lion and I'll be your guide throughout this book! I promise, by the end of this journey, you will get a deeper understanding of yourself, regardless of your sexual identity!"

Anonymous Artist
Mid-Night

Birthed black,
that was the definition of my skin;
no stars could be held there,
only dreams of grandeur within.
Tastes for the same scent,
that was the perversion of my heart; no antonyms could be held there,
no expected fever could set alight that path.
When my breath odored a testosterone stain
from magic merged in the drizzled rain, and my limbs upheld another
man's strain common to mine on Earth's singular plane, how could I claim
my history
or the future I was told I'd have to be?
For midnight,

for every beam of the moon's clandestine light that your hands' strokes softly highlight, I questioned my pulse, my destiny's plight: how could my heart not lead me right? Cloaked in another man's arms,
his archipelago of muscles disarm
any memory I had of identity.
Under that blank night sky, was I his only star? In the paralysis of passion, could we be who we are?
We sank into clear waters
when all was unclear,
baptismal in intent,
though reaffirming my despair;
without shadows, without fears,
sacred in twilight, barren of all cares, ignited, we stare,
me, sinking,
thinking the sea my savior,
prayers spent he couldn't hear.
I must kiss him softly.
Midnight, father of this epiphanic rite will guide our pathways through
light til we pronounce our heart tonight.
Inviting the sea's purging,
the shores yawn,
emerging,
I arise renewed,
waves surreptitiously urging
me forth,
reborn again a virgin
in the clasp of his hymnal might.
I must kiss him softly.
Midnight, father of this euphoric right will guide our pathways through
light til we pronounce our heart tonight.
Heaven, I am in love,
the organ flushes in proof.
Earth, my veins,
shall know no other truth.

Historically, and even in modern culture, the term "gay" has the power to strike an uncomfortable chord. Sometimes used as an insult, these three letters can incite such emotion as to provoke a violent response or promote psychological damage. Throughout the years, a word once used to refer to "happiness" has now grown into a title surrounded by stigma. When used in this manner, the label is a judgment on sexual orientation and used to describe homosexual men and women. Sexual Orientation is the physical and emotional allure that gears hormonal needs toward men, women, both or neither. It is important to understand the broadness of sexual orientation and that someone could be uninterested in sex, but still have a sexual orientation. American society has placed a heavy emphasis on sexuality, increasing confusion among adolescents and adults who don't "fit the norm." Some naturally question their orientation but limit their exploration based on discomfort enforced by culture.

To question your sexuality does not make you gay. There is no "Gay Test." Someone may question their sexuality based on: not feeling ready to be with anyone, a single deep connection with someone of the same gender, experiencing a random same-sex encounter sober or intoxicated, finding someone of the same sex physically attractive, having many gay friends, having homosexual relatives, etc.

"Remember, sexuality is fluid and you don't have to choose! Appreciating beauty in the human body just says you have good taste. Are you gay because you KNOW you look good? Not necessarily..."

Sexual identity is not something that can be easily boxed because it has many divisions and subdivisions. For example, there are those who consider themselves "heterosexuals that experience homosexual temptations." Assumptions of sexual identity should never be made on physical appearance. Many hold their sexual identification as highly as their racial and religious identity.

LGBT, LGBTQ, LGBTQIA, LGBTQ+, TBLG: These acronyms refer to Lesbian, Gay, Bisexual, Transgender, Queer or Questioning, Intersex, and Asexual or Ally. Although all of the different identities within "LGBT" are often lumped together (and share sexism as a common root of oppression), there are specific needs and concerns related to each individual identity. Similarly, it's important to not solely use LGBT acronyms to discuss sexual orientation, as many trans people are straight.

This list offers accepted definitions of sexual orientation and gender identity terms. This is not an exhaustive list, but rather, an introduction to language used within the community. For more information on accepted usage and terms to avoid, refer to "An Ally's Guide to Terminology," created by GLAAD (Gay & Lesbian Alliance Against Defamation).

Ally: Typically any non-LGBT person who supports and stands up for the rights of LGBT people, though LGBT people can be allies, such as a lesbian who is an ally to a transgender person.

Asexual: A person who generally does not feel sexual attraction or desire to any group of people. Asexuality is not the same as celibacy.

Bisexual: A person who is attracted to both people of their own gender and another gender.

Cisgender: A person whose personal gender identity matches their assigned sex at birth.

Coming out (of the closet): Describes when an LGBTQ person chooses to disclose their sexual orientation or gender identity.

Demisexual: A person whose sexual orientation is not limited by someone's gender and who only experiences sexual attraction once a strong emotional connection is formed.

Gay: A person who is attracted primarily to members of the same sex. Although it can be used for any sex (e.g., gay man, gay woman, gay person), "lesbian" is sometimes the preferred term for women who are attracted to women.

Gender expression: A term which refers to the ways in which we each manifest masculinity or femininity. It is usually an extension of our "gender identity," our innate sense of being male, female, etc. Each of us expresses a particular gender every day: by the way we style our hair, select our clothing, or even the way we stand. Our appearance, speech, behavior, movement, and other factors signal that we feel—and wish to be understood—as masculine or feminine, or as a man or a woman.

Gender fluid: A person who does not subscribe to a single gender and whose gender identity may shift is considered gender fluid.

Gender identity: The sense of "being" male, female, genderqueer, agender, etc. For some people, gender identity is in accord with physical anatomy. For transgender people, gender identity may differ from physical anatomy or expected social roles. It is important to note that gender identity, biological sex, and sexual orientation are separate and that you cannot assume how someone identifies in one category based on how they identify in another category.

Gender nonconforming (G.N.C.): When a person's gender expression does not conform to cultural or societal gender norms, such as "feminine" or "masculine."

Heterosexual: A person who is only attracted to members of the opposite sex. Also called "straight."

Homophobia: A range of negative attitudes and feelings toward homosexuality or people who are identified or perceived as being lesbian, gay, bisexual or transgender (LGBT). It can be expressed as antipathy, contempt, prejudice, aversion, or hatred, may be based on irrational fear, and is sometimes related to religious beliefs.

Homosexual: A clinical term for people who are attracted to members of the same sex. Some people find this term offensive. In the closet: Describes a person who keeps their sexual orientation or gender identity a secret from some or all people.

Intersex: A person born with variations of sexual characteristics, such as chromosomes, hormones, genitalia, etc, that defy standardized definitions of "male" and "female."

Lesbian: A woman who is primarily attracted to other women.

Nonbinary (or Genderqueer): A person whose gender identity is not exclusively female or male. The spectrum of nonbinary identities encompasses those outside of conventional gender binary, meaning that one may identify as both, neither, or a combination of genders.

Pansexual: A person who experiences sexual, romantic, physical, and/or spiritual attraction for members of all gender identities/expressions, not just people who fit into the standard gender binary (i.e., men, women, transgender, etc).

Queer: 1) An umbrella term sometimes used by LGBTQA people to refer to the entire LGBT community. 2) An alternative that some people use to "queer" the idea of the labels and categories such as lesbian, gay, bisexual, etc. It is important to note that the word queer is an in-group term, and a word that can be considered offensive to some people, depending on their generation, geographic location, and relationship with the word.

Questioning: For some, the process of exploring and discovering one's own sexual orientation, gender identity, or gender expression.

Sexual orientation: The type of sexual, romantic, and/or physical attraction someone feels toward others. Often labeled based on the gender identity/ expression of the person and who they are attracted to. Common labels: heterosexual, lesbian, gay, bisexual, pansexual, etc.

Transgender: This term has many definitions. It is frequently used as an umbrella term to refer to all people who do not identify with their assigned gender at birth or the binary gender system. This includes transsexuals, cross-dressers, genderqueer, drag kings, drag queens, and others. Some transgender people feel they exist not within one of the two standard gender categories, but rather somewhere between, beyond, or outside of those two genders.

Transphobia: The fear or hatred of transgender people or gender non-conforming behavior. Like biphobia, transphobia can also exist among lesbian, gay, and bisexual people as well as among heterosexual people.

Transsexual: A person whose gender identity is different from their biological sex, who may undergo medical treatments to change their biological sex, often times to align it with their gender identity, or they may live their lives as another sex.

Anonymous Artist
How did you come out?

My cousin invited me over and started asking me questions about this new club that was opened (gay club). She started asking me if I had heard about it and said that she knew [a] couple [of] my friends have been... Then she finally asked... I lied at first, however I finally gave in... She then said that I should tell my family, I said no. She insisted, then threatened me by saying if I didn't tell them she was... because they deserve to know... WTF???

Chapter 2

Is it Natural?

"I heard, from a very reliable source, that Male Amazon River dolphins... penetrate each other in the blowhole... LITERALLY."

The Core

The debate on whether sexuality is life choice or genetic disposition has gone on for centuries. It is a belief that if one wanted to switch their sexuality, they could by will, while others accept that sexuality is a natural instinct that individuals are born with. The second chapter of this book will focus on the origin of homosexuality and how natural, if at all, it actually is. So let us begin with nature. Other than humans, homosexuality and bisexuality have been recorded in over 400 species.[1]

"Call 'em out! This brings a whole new meaning to a Lion's PRIDE!"

Gay Animals

Non-reproductive sexual behavior commonly occurs in: Dolphins, Lions, Penguins, Dragonflies, Giraffes, Sheep, Swans, Dogs, Monkeys, Elephants, Foxes, Mallards, Apes, Pigeons, and many more.

Academic observations have shown that variations in sexual orientation or sexual preferences are present in several species. When given a choice, about 10% of rams will prefer to have intercourse with other rams rather than ewes.[2] Same sex relationships have appeared in a wide range of animals and have been recorded throughout history, but not publicized or pursued because of the ignominy surrounding the subject. Many biologists tried to explain away their research as meaningless—mainly because it defies their well known belief of Darwinism and procreation.

Biologist Janet Mann of Georgetown University recounts, "Scientists who study the topic are often accused of trying to forward an agenda, and their work can come under greater scrutiny than that of their colleagues who study other topics."[3]

For example, Joan Roughgarden challenged Darwin's concept of sexual selection in her book, *The Genial Gene: Deconstructing Darwinian Selfishness*. She presented the theory of "social-selection," which suggests these behaviors are bonding and fellowship rituals. Roughgarden announced 26 occurrences that supported social selection, rather than sexual selection.[4] Her ideas were severely criticized in the American Association for the Advancement of Science's (AAAS) academic journal—with more than a few distasteful remarks.

"The animal kingdom does it with much greater sexual diversity – including homosexual, bisexual and nonreproductive sex – than the scientific community and society at large have previously been willing to accept," quotes Bruce Bagemihl's *Biological Exuberance: Animal Homosexuality and Natural Diversity*. The book compiles various accounts of homosexual behavior in animals, but also exclaims that the findings have been downplayed over the past 150 years. Same-sex intercourse between animals was often referred to as "practice," "mock" or "nutritional." Some scientists even described this phenomenon as "a nuisance," while others simply ignored it.

Celebrity Quote
"At least 260 species of animals have been noted exhibiting homosexual behavior but only one species of animal ever, so far as we know, has exhibited homophobic behavior and that's the human being." **Stephen Fry**

Bagemihl exposed lapses in research by describing findings that recorded homosexual giraffe behavior, such as mounting and anal sex, as "greetings" and "dominance," but the same act on a female would simply be recorded as intercourse. Supporting Bagemihl, further evidence proved high homosexual giraffe activity. Some scientists now know giraffes to be "especially gay" due to a few studies that show up to 75% of their sexual behavior is either homosexual or bisexual.

"Wow, so sexuality can be nature's way of controlling a population. Never thought of it like that! Guess I should apologize to that rabbit that had a hare on his back! Thank you ladies, gentlemen, and everyone in-between, I'll be here the entire book! For more information on Homosexual animals, 'Against Nature?' is an exhibit found in the Natural History Museum, University of Oslo, Norway! Check it out!"

Like humans, the animal community has a variety of sexualities; certain animals can even change their gender at will. A common practice between fish and other sea creatures is to order a physical sex change when there is an imbalance within the population.

Female-to-male switches are called "protogyny," while male-to-female transformations, as we see in clownfish, are referred to as "protandry." These natural abilities are unique evolutionary traits that can be used to control overpopulation and benefit the ecosystem.

"My friend could have saved a lot of money, had she been born a clownfish!"

The Gay Brain

The World Health Organization (WHO) categorized homosexuality as a mental disorder until 1990, when the term was declassified. To mark this historic change, March 17th is considered the International Day against Homophobia, Transphobia and Biphobia. We have seen homosexuality occur in an abundance of beasts, yet animals often behave in ways humans do not. Let's examine Homo sapiens, a species known for its innate need to understand through categorization.

Despite subsequent efforts to "explain" homosexuality, scientists have failed to find a "gay gene." In fact, the 2019 large-scale study published in AAAS's (American Association for the Advancement of Science) *Science* journal affirmed that there is no conclusive gay gene. While we may attribute up to 25% of non-heterosexual behaviors to genetics, a whopping 75% is determined by environmental factors.

Hearsay suggests hormonal imbalances are responsible for sexual variation, but those studies have proved somewhat fruitless. Social psychologists, like Daryl Bem, have hypothesized that sexual orientation is determined indirectly by biology, but mainly originates from childhood experiences. He goes on to say that temperament and interest in gender-conforming or non-gender conforming activities can influence a child's orientation as an adult. This belief alludes to the theory that sexuality is based on an individual's environment. Sparking controversy, his theories have been misunderstood by some, blaming parents and suggesting sexuality is a habit that can be trained in and out of an individual.[5]

British-American neuroscientist, Simon LeVay, published the 1991 article "A difference in hypothalamic structure between heterosexual and homosexual men," which revealed key differences between heterosexual and homosexual brains. The third interstitial nucleus of the anterior hypothalamus (INAH3), is the sexually dimorphic nucleus (SDN) of the brain. Put shortly, it is a nest of cells associated with sexuality. The SDN was proven to be almost twice as large in heterosexual men than in homosexual and heterosexual female brains. LeVay accounted, "This finding indicates that INAH is dimorphic with sexual orientation, at least in men, and suggests that sexual orientation has a biological substrate."[6]

LeVay's work has been severely criticized by his colleagues, mainly because some of the brains used were from people who died of diseases. However, LeVay urges the understanding of his findings and states:

"It's important to stress what I didn't find. I did not prove that homosexuality is genetic, or find a genetic cause for being gay. I didn't show that gay men are born that way, the most common mistake people make in interpreting my work. Nor did I locate a gay center in the brain. The INAH3 is less likely to be the sole gay nucleus of the brain than a part of a chain of nuclei engaged in men and women's sexual behavior."

Research has also followed the differences in size of the INAH3 in direct relation to sexual activity in animals as well. Monkeys, rats, and otters have been known to behave according to the size of their SDN. Female-oriented rams, for example, tend to have a SDN nearly twice as large as male oriented rams, which is similar when compared to humans.[7][8]

"Here's food for thought: I always imagined it was more challenging for males to dominate other males rather than the 'weaker' sex... In some ways, does this make me more of a man?"

In 1992, 90 postmortem brains were examined by Laura Allen and Roger Gorski of UCLA. Within this collection of 30 heterosexual men, 30 heterosexual women, and 30 homosexual men, it was found that the all three brains had many differences, most notably, the size of the anterior commissure.[9]

The anterior commissure is a knot of nerve fibers that connects the left and right hemispheres of the brain. It joins the two amygdalae, which are partially responsible for the recognition of facial expressions, tones of voice, and body language.

Amygdalae are said to be more active in gay men, especially when sexual stimulation is introduced. The left and right temporal lobes are also connected by this structure. They contribute to the placement of meaningfulness, decision making, and processing sensory input. Together this system combined with the amygdalae enhances memory, instinct, intuition, emotion, speech, hearing and sexual behavior. Based on the studies of Allen and Gorski, homosexual males have an anterior commissure that is 18% larger than that of heterosexual women and 34% larger than the ones found in heterosexual male brains.[10]

"Extra connections help process the value of 'meaning' on the outside world or what I like to call, 'gaydar'!"

Similarly, Swedish scientists Ivanka Savic and Per Lindström revealed in 2008 that heterosexual men have a larger right hemisphere, while in women, both sides of the brain were relatively equal. The homosexual male brain was closer, in relation to size, to the heterosexual woman's brain. Homosexual women had brains that were fashioned more like heterosexual male brains. There are of course, studies that challenged these theories.[11] There is still much debate that surrounds the naturalness of sexuality and not enough study is conducted.

"The big question has always been the brains of gay men are different, or feminized, as earlier research suggests, then is it just limited to sexual preference or are there other regions that are gender atypical in gay males?" asks Dr. Eric Vilain, professor of human genetics at the University of California Los Angeles. "For the first time, in this study it looks like there are regions of the brain not directly involved in sexuality that seem to be feminized in gay males."

Anonymous Artist
When did you know?

I don't believe any events in life makes anybody gay or straight or whatever. I think when we are born our sexuality is already established just like the color of our eyes or skin are already established. I think we all just discover the sexuality that's already there whether we are aware of it or not.

I knew I had an attraction to other boys when I was young but I didn't pay it much mind until I got to high school and hot guys started flirting with me lol. My sexuality didn't change at all but the gay side that was already there kind of came to the forefront.

The Kinsey Scale

Created by American biologist Dr. Alfred Kinsey, the Kinsey Scale is a measurement system used to describe the sexual responses of a person at a given time. The scale ranges from 0, exclusively heterosexual, to 6, representing strictly homosexual preferences. The scale is a self-evaluation method that also includes a level "X" which marks asexual behaviors.

Through strenuous research, Kinsey and his team found that the sexuality of humans can change with time and vary in levels. Though the fluidity of sexual desire may fluctuate, most are found somewhere in-between 0 and 6. Written in *Sexual Behaviors in the Human Male*, he describes, "Males do not represent two discrete populations, heterosexual and homosexual. The world is not to be divided into sheep and goats…The living world is a continuum in each and every one of its aspects."

Kinsey expands later to describe in his book, S*exual Behavior of the Human Female*: "It is a characteristic of the human mind that tries to dichotomize in its classification of phenomena.... Sexual behavior is either normal or abnormal, socially acceptable or unacceptable, heterosexual or homosexual; and many persons do not want to believe that there are gradations in these matters from one to the other extreme."[12]

Since 1948, there have been advancements in the study of homosexuality and how it can be measured. Fritz Klein improved the scale with his "Klein Sexual Orientation Grid,"[13] which included specific relations to time such as: past, present, and ideal. For an even greater range of parameters, Michael D. Storms formed the "Storms model" that records eroticism on an X-Y grid.[14]

Celebrity Quote:
"I am who I am because of the people who influenced me growing up, and many of them were gay. No one has any right to tell anyone what makes a family." **Drew Barrymore**

Anonymous Artist
When did you know?

I am not attracted to dudes... I am attracted to a certain type of man first started with the anatomy/ his hips, thighs, to his character from understanding that in this lifestyle that there are a wide range of dudes from awkward and sometimes strange stages that attracts people for so many reasons even if they are some of the most stupidest and misunderstood.

Then in my situation becoming in the adult age of communication; I saw way beyond the anatomy, because even as a Top man, I got into my feelings, never thinking I could find the same thing in a man that I received in a woman.

This messed my head up; drawing me deeper in love, leading me right back to his irresistibleness that felt no different than a woman. Although I tried to fight it and leave him alone due to acceptance and paranoia.

I then became assuredly comfortable because he was that dude who was thick like a chick, but mad masculine and made me see that you don't have to be fem to take on his position or be out on the scene. He genuinely loved me and treated me better than my wife. By that, I was satisfied and after we really got deep; we ended up understanding that it was hard to play both sides of the field and maintain our love and deep emotions for one another.

Simply, "Because I was not attracted to dudes in no kinda way and he introduced me to this and we had history already, the transition and choices made were easy without the blame game." I loved him, that's what got me here in the lifestyle.

At the highest of the animal hierarchy we know whether certain conduct, though it be natural, is polite, acceptable, or publicly shameful. Belching, scratching, and smelling are all behaviors that occur naturally, as well as mental health disorders such as kleptomania, necrophilia, and pedophilia. Though we share the same habitual needs with many animals, there is an obvious line crossed when that need harms another individual.

This is why Homo sapiens have created law. Law provides structure to the sometimes harmful instinctive actions that can occur with the human race. It protects us from harming one another. Law should not punish individuals for acts that are harmless and natural—such as yelling, sleeping, or desiring a same sex partner—but should continue to focus on protecting all citizens from danger.

Anonymous Artist
When did you know?

I've always liked other boys since I was little. Around the age of 5 or 6. I liked both guys and girls, but [now] I only get down with the fellas. In my case, all I can say is that I was born this way. So I guess it happened naturally. No one made me this way. I have 2 other brothers and they don't get down... same parents, same lifestyle... different outcomes. I find it sometimes hard to believe that lack of a father-figure is what makes someone gay.

That's ridiculous because of all those fatherless people walking around and are not gay. I think it may have helped contribute, but wasn't a big factor.

Chapter 3

Gayness in History

Where did homosexuality originate and how did it evolve through time?

"Someone once told me that the Ancient Greeks invented it because they thought women were UNCLEAN and should only be used for procreation. ...Well that's just rude. Silly humans. My how times have changed!"

Origins

Homosexuality began with the creation of sex. Humankind, as a whole, has changed its overall opinion on homosexuality several times throughout history. Same sex relations have gone from widely encouraged to just accepted and eventually, in some societies, an executional crime. Past views on sexuality were never set in stone, as many preferences were on a case by case basis. Historical figures like Alexander the Great, William Shakespeare, and Socrates were all known for sexual diversity.

In 12th century England, the word "gay" rooted from the French word, "gai," which meant "joyful" or "bright and showy." Around the 17th century, however, the word was commonly linked to dishonorable conduct, overindulgence, promiscuity, and a carefree temperament. The term "gay it" arose in the 19th century, which meant "to have sex" and, ironically, alluded to a man who had many female partners. It wasn't until the 1950s when the word became what it means today.

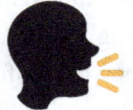

Celebrity Quote
"When women got the vote, they did not redefine voting. When African Americans got the right to sit at a lunch counter alongside White people, they did not redefine eating out. They were simply invited to the table. That is all we want to do; we have no desire to change marriage. We want to be entitled to not only the same privileges but the same responsibilities as straight people." **Cynthia Nixon**

Africa

Early accounts of homosexuality were first recorded in Egypt. Much debate surrounds the relationship between Khnumhotep and Niankhkhnumm, "royal confidants" often depicted in the "nose kissing position," one of the most intimate Egyptian poses. There are arguments that state the two are simply twin brothers as they both were reported to have wives. Some even say that they are gay twin brothers. The theories vary depending on who you ask. However, as discussed previously in this chapter, sexuality was never a permanent stamp; like today, many gay men and women did and can produce offspring, some even have straight spouses.

Many tend to blame homosexuality in Africa on the influence of European civilizations. This placement of fault is wrong and, as further information suggests, has always been a myth. The San Bushmen people of Southern Africa immortalized pictures of men having sex with other men, which told stories of their sexual freedoms.

Anthropologists, including E. E. Evans-Pritchard, who is best known for his work with the Azande culture, have documented several queer acts among natives. According to Evans-Pritchard's findings, male warriors would often take on other men to perform duties usually assigned to the wife, which included sexually pleasing their husband, preparing food, and watching children. Often referring to these men as "boy-wives," Evans-Pritchard stated:

"Homosexuality is indigenous. Azande do not regard it as at all improper, indeed as very sensible for a man to sleep with boys when women are not available or are taboo… In the past this was a regular practice at court. Some princes may even have preferred boys to women, when both were available. This is not a question I can enter into further here beyond saying I was told that some princes sleep with boys before consulting poison oracles, women being then taboo, and also that they sometimes do so on other occasions, just because they like them."[15]

Nowadays, LGBT views in Africa have completely changed. As of 2020, it is a criminal act in 35 African countries and punishable by a lifetime imprisonment or death in Mauritania, northern Nigeria, southern Somalia, and Sudan. Nigeria has also extended the law to straight family members and friends anyone "who administers, witnesses, abets or aids" same sex unions with at least a 10-year jail sentence.

Many leaders believe it is against their culture, religion and nature, even though history has proven otherwise. Currently, there are 19 African countries where homosexuality is legal. South Africa, the most liberal country, has progressively recognized same-sex marriage and is the only African nation to do so.[16]

North America

Before the arrival of the pilgrims, most Native American tribes clung to the idea of three to four genders: Masculine man, feminine man, masculine woman, and feminine woman.[17] For cultures such as the Zuni, it did not matter which biological sex a child was born because the decision of gender identity was made by that person around the age of puberty. Depending on who you asked, early homosexuals were considered "Two-Spirited," "lhamana,"or "berdache" and had mixed gender roles. Common practices of the lhamana included cross dressing and domestic tasks.

Two-Spirit peoples were respected and considered valuable to society. They were thought to be a complete human, as they possessed attributes from both sexes. Often healers, spiritual guides, match-makers, fortune-tellers, and artists, the lhamana served as sources of intelligence and style. This was because they doubled the work of female assigned tasks such as millwork and performed male duties when warriors went off to battle. Two-Spirits were men regarded with respect; however, they were never immune to the law and, like all medicine men, were sometimes accused of witchcraft and killed when the tribe suffered great misfortunes.[18]

Since colonization, views on homosexuality have varied based on jurisdiction, but it was unpopular as a whole. Gay rights came into question around 1950 when the Under Secretary of State, James E. Webb, commented on gay men and women stating, "It is generally believed that those who engage in overt acts of perversion lack the emotional stability of normal persons." Shortly after, homosexuality was considered a mental disorder brought on by scarring parent-child histories and fear of the opposite sex.[19]

Celebrity Quote

"At some point in our lifetime, gay marriage won't be an issue, and everyone who stood against this civil right will look as outdated as George Wallace standing on the school steps keeping James Hood from entering the University of Alabama because he was Black."
George Clooney

The NYPD preformed regular "sweeps" of the neighborhood where they often arrested and publicly humiliated gays and those that were suspected of gay behavior. Men dressed as women were jailed on sight. Many were fired from their jobs, thrown out of their homes, and placed in mental institutions or prisons. Alternatively, they lived double lives and patronized undercover mafia and mob owned businesses. These secret bars and clubs were frequent targets for police, but the rich proprietors could often afford to pay off raids.

June 28, 1969, reports a significant mark in gay history when a raid went wrong. The Stonewall Inn, a gay bar on Christopher Street (located in the West Village neighborhood of Manhattan) was made famous for being one of the first to allow male-on-male dancing. This rare attraction made enough money to survive raids. One night at Stonewall, tensions between the police, mafia members, and the bar guests boiled with rumors of refusal to pay or a transaction gone wrong. Stonewall Inn was soon raided and several homosexuals were beaten and detained. However, unlike in previous sweeps, this time the crowd fought back. Pent up emotions were finally released when pushing and shoving became vandalizing and rioting. Violence spread throughout the streets as glass shattered and fires raged. It was one of the few times police were overrun and forced to retreat. The upheaval sparked several other heated riots and brawls that subsequently occurred.[20]

"Hell hath no fury like Homosexual scorned..."

When word had gotten to the press, the news of the riots promoted a need for homosexual unification. The Gay Liberation Front (GLF) was the first organization to boldly form with the mission to protect homosexuals from unjust treatment and prosecution. Support of their peaceful marches grew, and the GLF gained an interesting political platform that commented on discrimination as a whole. This gave room for other gay associations to manifest on a worldwide scale. A year later on Christopher Street Liberation Day (June 28, 1970), supporters performed the first Gay Pride march, which is now an annual tradition.[21]

Celebrity Quote
"It is each American's constitutional right to marry the person they love, no matter what state they inhabit. No state should decide who can marry and who cannot. Thanks to the tireless work of so many, someday soon this discrimination will end and every American will be able to enjoy their equal right to marriage." **Brad Pitt**

In the United States, the availability of legally-recognized same-sex marriage expanded from one state in 2004 to all 50 states in 2015 through various state and federal court rulings, state legislation, and direct popular votes.

As of June 26, 2015, all 50 U.S. states recognize gay marriage. Adoption rules vary by state based on marriage laws. However, there are states that have the option of a same-sex union, which offers some but not all of the legal advantages that pertain to marriage. It is not ideal, but is certainly a step in the right direction.

East Asia

Homosexuality in East Asia has existed long since the country's written word. Ancient Asian art revealed recurring intimate relationships between homosexuals with the same regard as it did with straight couples. Gayness in males was referenced in poetry and stories as "the bitten peach" and was as neutral as the words for "wind" or "water."[22] It has always been a norm in China, and some literature has even expressed the act as more pleasurable than heterosexual relationships. Favored among emperors and other great leaders, the practice of bisexuality was never frowned upon until, some debate, Western influence.[23]

In the 20th century, the Republic of China prohibited sodomy all together and it became punishable by jail time. This ban wasn't lifted until 1997, and by 2001, homosexuality was no longer considered a mental illness.[24] In 2018, China took LGBT rights a step further and prohibited sexual orientation reversal therapy. Like China, Japan had similar views in regard to alternative lifestyles. In fact, some Buddhist organizations were well-known for same sex interactions, and non-Buddhist religious showed no criticism. Male relationships were considered sacred and honored. Older traditions supported male bonding and respected it as an eternal commitment.

Commonly, samurai warriors would take on a younger male apprentice. Through the practice of shudō, these two would share a lifelong bond and defend each other during life-threatening missions. They were also known to be lovers. Free to also engage in heterosexual interactions, the apprentice could find other mates but never divert from his master until he came of skill and age.[25]

In 1872, anal sodomy was banned in Japan and revoked only eight years later. Japan now provides laws that protect gay and transgender people. Political history notes Aya Kamikawa as the first transgender elected official to take seat at the Setagaya ward in Tokyo. An example of prestige to her class, she was re-elected in 2007 and based her work on protecting the rights of women, children, persons with disabilities, and, of course, the LGBT community. Though the government continued to consider her a male, she announced she will always work as a woman.

Celebrity Quote
Discussing New York legalizing gay marriage
"I was stoked that that happened. ... We're people and we're different, all of us. And we should be using our differences to bring ourselves closer together. You know? Not be afraid of something that we don't know. ... It's unfortunate that things take a while to progress like this, but it was a great, great victory for equality. I'm proud New York has the balls to stand up for what's right." **Justin Timberlake**

Europe

Not many can argue the rampant homosexuality in Ancient Greece. Most emperors of Rome and other regions were reported to take on male lovers. Mythology told many stories surrounding male bonds, which famously included: Achilles and Patroclus, Hercules and Abderus, and Apollo the Greek god with the Spartan prince Hyacinthus. Greek views on sexuality had less to do with gender and focused more on passive and possessive roles. For example, regardless of who was engaging in intercourse, the penetrator was always thought to be more masculine and of higher social status, while the penetrated was considered submissive and more feminine.

**Greek Myth:
Zeus and Ganymede**

According to legend, Tros of Troy had a son named Ganymede who was said to be one of the most attractive boys at that time. Ganymede grew up to be a sheepherder and even the mighty Zeus admired his beauty. One day while he tended to his animals, a giant eagle flew down in the midst of a sudden thunderstorm. The eagle captured Ganymede and revealed himself as the mighty god once they got to Mount Olympus. Infatuated with his new lover, Zeus granted Ganymede immortality and made him the cupbearer to the gods. All the gods were said to applaud Ganymede's grace except for Hera, Zeus's wife. She insisted her husband's love for the man was tiresome and was extremely jealous. Like any good father would, Tros became grief-stricken over his missing son. Understanding his loss, Zeus sent Hermes with magical horses that would never die and could walk on water. Hermes explained to Tros that his son was now the cupbearer of the gods and Zeus hoped that these horses would ease the pain… But he wasn't getting Ganymede back. Ganymede was said to live a happy life. Zeus was so appreciative of his love that he eventually placed him among the stars as the constellation: Aquarius, the water bearer.

Though homosexual couples, such as Pausanias of Athens and poet Agathon were accepted, masculinity was a prized quality, and feminine men were socially ridiculed. In the past, manliness was equated with power. History tells that Roman soldiers were prohibited from marriage under Augustus but were allowed to have sexual relations with male slaves and prostitutes. Same-sex relations between soldiers were strictly outlawed as it was believed that a penetrated man lost his masculinity and should not be a soldier.

"Ancient 'don't ask don't tell.' Whoever said history doesn't repeat itself."

Once Christianity became the official faith of Rome, social opinions about same-sex unions turned sour and became punishable by death. Such murders included burning and public castration of both partners. Sodomy became a huge crime in Europe and was only decriminalized by Poland in 1932.[26] As time passed, Sweden, like many countries in Europe, included homosexuality on its mental illness list, until 1979, when hundreds of residents called out sick from work because they "felt gay."[27] Only a few months later, homosexuality was removed from this list, and in 2009, the Church of Sweden gave its blessing to homosexual couples, including support of marriage. The Netherlands was the first European country to recognize gay marriage, and now, as of 2019, 18 out of 44 European countries have legalized same-sex marriage. Another 11 recognize civil unions, but not marriage. The remaining 22, including the Vatican, do not support same-sex marriage or civil unions.

Middle East

Thought to be an affront to Allah, homosexuality has been illegal for centuries in nearly all of the Islamic States, chiefly those that maintain Sharia-based criminal laws. Believed to be brought on by Western influence, the crime is still punishable by death in Afghanistan, Iran, Saudi Arabia, and Yemen. Few laws exist preventing hate-crimes or discrimination against LGBT people, though Sudan, which formerly recognized homosexuality as a capital offense, revised its legislature in 2020 to ban the death penalty as well as flogging.

Same-sex relations continue to be a very touchy subject as governments have been accused of secretly trying to exterminate their gay communities, while others claim these arrests and deaths were made based on rape and drug trafficking violations.

Homosexuality was legalized in Israel in 1988, and in 1992, same-sex couples were allowed to adopt children and join the military. The magazine *Out* has considered Israel the "gay capital of the Middle East," as they annually celebrate Pride and continue to make powerful strides in a more accepting direction.

Even though punishments of stoning, torture, imprisonment, and even death are possible, there are still gay individuals who take the risk. In 2005, Saudi police arrested 110 men for attending a secret gay wedding party. Gays are known to collect around certain malls and grocery stores, and these gay hotspots are subject to government raids. Because the crime of homosexuality needs no evidence or trial, legal enforcers have conducted murder on the assumption of homosexuality alone.[28]

Chapter 4

What Religion Has to Say

Across the world, religion and government have shared a complicated relationship. Though some regions often emphasize the separation of church and state, it is clear that the two influence one another and together shape public opinion. Through the passing of laws and religious attitudes, societal views on the subject of homosexuality have often been affected negatively. Now we will discuss religious views on the gay scene.

Buddhism

Generally, overindulgence, material pleasures, and sexual misconduct are all against Buddhist ethics. "Sexual misconduct" has been defined in many ways. Buddhism supports elevating beyond the need of all sensual desires, which include both homosexual and heterosexual desires. Buddhists have different sets of rules for monks and someone who is considered a layperson (a man or woman who lived outside the temple). Buddha himself has never commented on homosexuality.

Many interpreters believe he considered all sexuality equal and should abide by the same principles.[30] Some zones such as Thailand don't necessarily disagree, but insinuate that through reincarnation, returning as a homosexual is a karmic retribution for sexual sins committed as a heterosexual. Because of this, gay rights in Theravada Buddhist countries have not improved past cultural norms. The Dalai Lama has mentioned that from a Buddhist point of view, gay sex, like all sex, is considered sexual misconduct, but from a society's viewpoint, they can be "of mutual benefit, enjoyable, and harmless."

Christianity

The New Encyclopedia of Britannica referred to the Bible as "the most influential collection of books in human history." Christianity has many branches and all believe the Bible is their holiest text. For most, it is a guide for life. It sets a standard of living by teaching lessons through stories. There are many different translations, versions, and edits that have been made to the Bible, however, and when it comes to homosexuality, these passages stick out:

"God blessed them and said to them, 'Be fruitful and increase in number; fill the earth and subdue it. Rule over the fish of the sea and the birds of the air and over every living creature that moves on the ground." (Genesis 1:28)

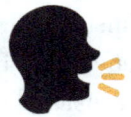

Celebrity Quote
"Make no mistake—I am a Christian and I believe in God and I don't believe he makes mistakes, so I believe that being gay is not a sin and in fact it's how you're made." **Kristin Chenoweth**

"'Be fruitful and increase in numbers' was great back in the day when medicine was weak and they died at 32, but now the earth has about oh... 7 BILLION people on it."

"Do not lie with a man as one lies with a woman; that is detestable." (Leviticus 18:22) "If a man lies with a man as one lies with a woman, both of them have done what is detestable. They must be put to death; their blood will be on their own heads." (Leviticus 20:13)

Because of the social highlights on the gay movement, it is regularly forgotten or ignored that the Bible also proclaims:

"These shall ye eat of all that are in the waters: whatsoever hath fins and scales in the waters, in the seas, and in the rivers, they shall ye eat. And all that have not fins and scales in the seas, and in the rivers, of all that move in the waters, and of any living thing which is in the waters, they shall be an abomination unto you: They shall be even an abomination unto you; ye shall not eat of their flesh, but ye shall have their carcasses in abomination. Whatsoever hath no fins nor scales in the waters, that shall be an abomination unto you." (Leviticus 11:9-12)

Then in Deuteronomy 14:9-10, "These ye shall eat of all that are in the waters: all that have fins and scales shall ye eat: And whatsoever hath not fins and scales ye may not eat; it is unclean unto you."

"I always knew Red Lobster was the devil's work! Those biscuits are sinful!"

As with most things, the Bible is left to be interpreted by those who choose to read it. Matthew 8:5-13 explains a controversial story which has raised questions about the heroic figure Jesus Christ and his opinion on homosexuality. Here is a translation of the tale:

When Jesus had entered Capernaum, a centurion came to him, asking for help. "Lord," he said, "my servant lies at home paralyzed, suffering terribly."

Jesus said to him, "Shall I come and heal him?"

The centurion replied, "Lord, I do not deserve to have you come under my roof. But just say the word, and my servant will be healed. For I myself am a man under authority, with soldiers under me. I tell this one, 'Go,' and he goes; and that one, 'Come,' and he comes. I say to my servant, 'Do this,' and he does it."

When Jesus heard this, he was amazed and said to those following him, "Truly I tell you, I have not found anyone in Israel with such great faith. I say to you that many will come from the east and the west, and will take their places at the feast with Abraham, Isaac and Jacob in the kingdom of heaven. But the subjects of the kingdom will be thrown outside, into the darkness, where there will be weeping and gnashing of teeth."

Then Jesus said to the centurion, "Go! Let it be done just as you believed it would." And his servant was healed at that moment."

Translated from Greek, this story first used the word "pais" to describe the sick slave. Pais, which meant "same-sex lover" or "servant," implied a sexual relationship between the two. This would mean that Jesus blessed a gay couple.

Debaters have taken this passage under several microscopes and still disagree, maintaining that since the Bible was edited by men, it makes sense that the stories pertained as lessons for those times and that edits can sometimes be individual interpretations. Others insist the centurion had a wife and children and therefore wasn't gay.⁽³¹⁾

> "Never have I heard masters LOVING their slaves that much... Something else must have been going on..."

Most Protestant churches have used these unclear scriptures as the force behind their homophobic tendencies. In many forms of Christianity, the idea that homosexuality is sinful is prominent. The Southern Baptist Convention reinforces that sexuality is a choice and can be overcome by chastity. Mormon and Jehovah's Witnesses churches have also supported this belief.

While the Roman Catholic Church opens doors to homosexuals, it teaches the sinfulness of the act. Fractions of Christianity, such as in Lutheranism and Methodism churches, divide when it comes to same sex acceptance and marriage—overall, the judgment less preferred. Liberal Christians have supported the Metropolitan Community Church and the United Church of Christ as well as some Anglican and Lutheran cathedrals, which all bless gay unions.⁽³²⁾

Hinduism

Like in most cultures, public opinions of gay men and women ranged from favorable to detested. Homosexuality has become an uncomfortable subject among the religious, while Hindu texts surround the subject with obscurity. Though early Indian recordings such as the Kama Sutra depicted both gay and lesbian carvings, modern day Hindus rarely talk about it. Numerous opposing views exist, as the ancient Hindu doctrines never excluded homosexuals from romantic love, only looked down upon sexual overindulgence. All that was required for marriage was for the two individuals to share these requirements:

Dharma: duty, harmony, balance
Artha: worldly possessions/wealth
Kama: passion, lust, desire
Moksha: spiritual liberation, enlightenment

"Hinduism recognizes a "third gender" too! These were people who didn't fit into their gender norms!"

Anonymous Artist
How did your family react?

My mother has known about me since I was a teenager, when people started having the net at home (and) we got a computer. That was when the page would slowly load instead of popping right up. I thought I cut the computer off but I didn't and it froze with half a picture on the screen. A naked guy.

She didn't say anything until I sent someone a message about how good this cute dude was and I sent it to my mother by mistake. For some reason I didn't realize I entered her number instead of my friend's. She sent me a reply that said "Did you mean to send this to your mother." I was really embarrassed and at the time I just happened to be on my way to her house. I thought about not going but I went, she was cool, didn't mention it and everything was normal.

In mythology, many gods were known to be bisexual, change gender, and even have children with a like-sexed god. Hindus believed in the naturalness of sexuality but questioned its purpose and righteousness. Homosexuals are not damned because of their birth, as in some cultures. They are believed to share a part of the divine, like every other soul.[33]

Gay men and women have been married under Hindu ceremonies, while there are more Christianized Hindus who refused to acknowledge their existence. Modern day standpoints are usually split down the middle. *Dancing with Śiva: Hinduism's Contemporary Catechism* (1991) was written by Satguru Sivaya, a highly respected guru. The book reads, "Sons and daughters who are gay may not benefit from marriage, and should be taught to remain loyal in relationships and be prepared to cope with community challenges."[34]

Celebrity Quote
"Equality. Absolutely. That's what defines us. It's what makes us great. If it doesn't sit well with your religion, let your God sort it out in the end, but that's us. We're equal." **Brad Pitt**

Islam

Muslims cultures strictly forbid homosexuality, making the act, in countries such as Afghanistan, Brunei, and Iran, punishable by death. All Islamic schools, with the exception of a handful, have condemned same-sex relations. The disposition is rooted in their book of worship and embedded into their culture. The Qur'an reprimands homosexuality completely. Such stories as "The People of Lut" ("The Story of Lot") or "Sodom and Gomorrah" have told of God's swift and destructive vengeance against towns that practice immoral behavior.[35]

Anonymous Artist

Sitting up in my room, thinking of suicide Staring at the knife, I really hate my life I look back and discover, I accomplished nothing
it's what the voice inside tells me
suicide will put an end to the hurt, pain and suffering
Lights turned down, here in the dark Holding onto the knife that will take it all away
none of these people i think of, don't care when I think of myself, i'm so ashamed
knife run cross my skin
As I watch the blood pour out
I ain't fading quick enough
So I make a few more attempts
before i made the final attempt
by stabbing myself in the heart

"I remember there being a lot more going on than just homosexuality in Sodom and Gomorrah..."

In some nations, strong communal opinions often erupt into violence. Gays have been publicly beaten, stoned, and burned. Anti-gay protesters have combed the streets, rioted, and taken the law into their own hands. Homophobia has gained such strength in Muslim countries it has caused paranoia. In 2007, two Moroccan men were sentenced to jail time after being caught in a car together. "We were in the car having a chat, nothing more. We've done nothing illegal," quoted the defendant. Their lawyer explained the arrest as a punishment for being homosexual.[36]

Article 489 of the Moroccan penal code makes homosexuals vulnerable to a maximum of a three year jail sentence.[37]

Celebrity Quote
"Being gay is not a crime" **Charlamagne tha God**

Chapter 5
Homophobia

"If you fear something you're letting it have power over you. ...I don't mind having power! I just have to learn how to use it..."

Power of Fear

Homophobia, defined by Webster's dictionary as an irrational fear of, aversion to, or discrimination against homosexuality or homosexuals, has been at the root of emotional enigmas and various violent vendettas. Historically, underlying homophobia has negatively informed political decisions, family choices, and social attitudes, hurting many and even causing some to take their own lives. Whether you agree or not, I hope we can come to a conclusion that suicide and murder are wrong.

Like with most phobias, the fear lies in ignorance. Not knowing about something can certainly make it scary. With phobias, such as scopophobia, the fear of being looked at critically, and agoraphobia, the fear of leaving the house, most psychologists suggest publicly experiencing time with said fear. This begins a learning process that teaches the irrationality of harmless phobias. Being homophobic does not make anyone more straight. In fact, there have been recent studies that confirm homophobic tendencies are more prominent in those who have suppressed homosexual desires. As seen in history, homophobia has caused witch hunts, suspicion, and upheaval. Here are some commonly believed gay myths, rooted in our culture.

Gone Too Soon

Jamey Rodemeyer, Buffalo, New York was a 14-year-old blogger who struggled with his sexuality. He was a popular target for bullies and thereby was consistently taunted. Distraught and tormented, Jamey spoke out through his blogs. However, bullies took this opportunity to abuse him virtually with comments such as, "JAMIE IS STUPID, GAY, FAT AND UGLY! HE MUST DIE!" and "I wouldn't care if you died. No one would. So just do it. :) It would make everyone WAY more happier!"

In his final post, Jamey wrote, "No one in my school cares about preventing suicide, while you're the ones calling me a faggot and tearing me down." Jamey was found dead that Sunday morning.

8 Common Gay Myths

1. One homosexual experience can make you gay! My roommate once got drunk and slept with her best friend! GAY.

WRONG. A single sexual experience does not determine sexuality. Nor does a dream or fantasy. As described in previous chapters, sexuality is fluid and never clear cut. It is completely possible for someone to engage in homosexual activity but still consider themselves straight. Many teens and young adults, naturally, go through experimentation phases where sexuality is tested and later determined by the individual.

2. All Gays are Pedophiles!

WRONG. Though no one can deny, pedophilia is a problem among heterosexual and homosexual individuals regardless of race or creed. The majority of child molestation cases are heterosexual, and research proves homosexuals are responsible for less than a third of these crimes. In 1992, an exploratory study from scientist Kurt Freund required male participants to look at pictures of naked children. By measuring penile bloodflow, he found the reactions of heterosexual and homosexual men as generally the same.[38]

3. Gays could never be good parents! It'll confuse the child and stunt their growth!

WRONG. "The bottom line is that the science shows that children raised by two same gender parents do as well on average as children raised by two different-gender parents," quotes Timothy Biblarz, a sociologist at the University of Southern California. "This is obviously inconsistent with the widespread claim that children must be raised by a mother and a father to do well."[39] In the world's largest comparison of children raised by same-sex couples and children raised by heterosexual partners in 2013, on average, children from same-sex couples did better academically and were less likely to shoplift and get into trouble.[40]

4. Every gay man wants a straight man! All the gays want to do is turn everyone on to their sick queer agenda!

WRONG. Just as every straight man isn't attracted to every woman, gays aren't attracted to every man. Gays have a wide list of preferences and a large part of that is geared toward more feminine men.

Gone Too Soon

If you are reading this, it means that I have committed suicide and obviously failed to delete this post from my queue. Please don't be sad, it's for the better. The life I would've lived isn't worth living in... because I'm transgender. I could go into detail explaining why I feel that way, but this note is probably going to be lengthy enough as it is. To put it simply, I feel like a girl trapped in a boy's body, and I've felt that way ever since I was 4. I never knew there was a word for that feeling, nor was it possible for a boy to become a girl, so I never told anyone and I just continued to do traditionally "boyish" things to try to fit in.

When I was 14, I learned what transgender meant and cried of happiness. After 10 years of confusion I finally understood who I was. I immediately told my mom, and she reacted extremely negatively, telling me that it was a phase, that I would never truly be a girl, that God doesn't make mistakes, that I am wrong. If you are reading this, parents, please don't tell this to your kids. Even if you are Christian or that won't do anything but make them hate them self. That's exactly what it did to me.

My mom started taking me to a therapist, but would only take me to Christian therapists (who were all very biased), so I never actually got the therapy I needed to cure me of my depression. I only got more Christians telling me that I was selfish and wrong and that I should look to God for help.

When I was 16 I realized that my parents would never come around, and that I would have to wait until I was 18 to start any sort of transitioning treatment, which absolutely broke my heart. The longer you wait, the harder it is to transition. I felt hopeless, that I was just going to look like a man in drag for the rest of my life. On my 16th birthday, when I didn't receive consent from my parents to start transitioning, I cried myself to sleep. I formed a sort of a "fuck you" attitude towards my parents and came out as gay at school, thinking that maybe if I eased into coming out as trans it would be less of a shock.
Although the reaction from my friends was positive, my parents were pissed. They felt like I was attacking their image, and that I was an embarrassment to them. They wanted me to be their perfect little straight Christian boy, and that's obviously not what I wanted.
So they took me out of public school, took away my laptop and phone, and forbid me of getting on any sort of social media, completely isolating me from my friends. This was probably the part of my life when I was the most depressed, and I'm surprised I didn't kill myself. I was completely alone for 5 months. No friends, no support, no love. Just my parent's disappointment and the cruelty of loneliness.

At the end of the school year, my parents finally came around and gave me my phone and let me back on social media. I was excited, I finally had my friends back. They were extremely excited to see me and talk to me, but only at first. Eventually they realized they didn't actually give a shit about me, and I felt even lonelier than I did before. The only friends I thought I had only liked me because they saw me five times a week.

After a summer of having almost no friends plus the weight of having to think about college, save money for moving out, keep my grades up, go to church each week and feel like shit because everyone there is against everything I live for, I have decided I've had enough. I'm never going to transition successfully, even when I move out. I'm never going to be happy with the way I look or sound. I'm never going to have enough friends to satisfy me. I'm never going to have enough love to satisfy me. I'm never going to find a man who loves me. I'm never going to be happy. Either I live the rest of my life as a lonely man who wishes he were a woman or I live my life as a lonelier woman who hates herself. There's no winning. There's no way out. I'm sad enough already, I don't need my life to get any worse. People say "it gets better" but that isn't true in my case. It gets worse. Each day I get worse.

That's the gist of it, that's why I feel like killing myself. Sorry if that's not a good enough reason for you, it's good enough for me. As for my will, I want 100% of the things that I legally own to be sold and the money (plus my money in the bank) to be given to trans civil rights movements and support groups, I don't give a shit which one.
The only way I will rest in peace is if one day transgender people aren't treated the way I was, they're treated like humans, with valid feelings and human rights. Gender needs to be taught about in schools, the earlier the better. My death needs to mean something. My death needs to be counted in the number of transgender people who commit suicide this year. I want someone to look at that number and say "that's fucked up" and fix it. Fix society. Please.

Goodbye,
Leelah Acorn (Suicide Note)

5. Gays were molested as kids! That's why they're gay!

WRONG. Homosexuality is not a disease you can catch. Nor is it an illness brought down by psychological damage. No research has even been shown to support this. Such claims further stereotypes, breed shame, and empower hatred. Specified by the National Organization on Male Sexual Victimization, "experts in the human sexuality field do not believe that premature sexual experiences play a significant role in late adolescent or adult sexual orientation." They believe it is impossible that anyone can make another person gay or heterosexual.

6. But if we let up on homosexuality, what's next?! The legalization of bestiality?! Necrophilia?!

WRONG. Heterosexuality, homosexuality, and bisexuality are all sexual orientations. Sexual orientation alone does not harm anyone and is far from abusive. Society is not harmed if two consenting sound-minded adults make the decision to have a relationship. It is of course the duty of the individual regardless of orientation to engage in sex responsibly.

7. You cannot be born gay!

WRONG. Various scientific theories suggest that homosexuality is based on a number of biological and environmental influences. In 2008, the largest study of twins published in the peer-reviewed journal *Archives of Sexual Behavior* argued that fraternal twins often share the same sexual orientation, suggesting more biological links to sexuality. The American Psychological Association has even reported that "homosexual orientation is in place very early in the life cycle, possibly even before birth."[41] Many gays claim to have known their orientation at a young age, often before puberty.

8. Even if you're born gay, you can still change it!

WRONG. This debate has gone on for too long. Countless agreements state that homosexuality can be cured. Supporters believe it can be prayed, trained, or simply willed out. Exodus International was one of the largest ex-gay ministries. Its mission was to change the sexuality of people through conversion therapy. Exodus consisted of 120 ministers in the United States and over 150 in Canada with the slogan, "Change is possible!"

Founded in 1976, Exodus was dissolved in 2013 after its director and now activist, Alan Chambers, issued a statement, "The majority of people that I have met, and I would say the majority meaning 99.9% of them, have not experienced a change in their orientation or have gotten to a place where they could say they could never be tempted or are not tempted in some way or experience some level of same-sex attraction."

He goes on to apologize, "I am sorry for the pain and hurt many of you have experienced. I am sorry that some of you spent years working through the shame and guilt you felt when your attractions didn't change. I am sorry we promoted sexual orientation change efforts and reparative theories about sexual orientation that stigmatized parents."

Celebrity Quote
"I think that it is a good time for those who voted for the ban against gay marriage to sit and reflect and anticipate their great shame and the

> shame in their grandchildren's eyes if they continue that way of support. We've got to have equal rights for everyone." **Sean Penn**

At the end of the day, no one would willingly choose to have their basic human rights questioned and the nature of their existence hated. Belief systems that support these ideas increase shame and do more harm to a society than good. Sexual orientation, like the color of your skin, is part of your genetic code and can never truly be changed.

Anonymous Artist
Lessons

I met this dude the day before my B'day last year and I went to his house. He was a lil Thug boy. Should I drop his name?
Anyway... we did it everywhere. In public restrooms... At the Club... and anywhere else we went.

Then after that it all just went downhill. About a month later I tested positive for HIV. It could've been this guy I met. But it showed up a month later. Could it have been someone else. My eyes got really puffy and I could not stop coughing. I was diagnosed with CAP, Community Acquired Pneumonia. They gave me antibiotics and released me after 3 days.

I started to break out in real bad forehead acne for about six months before deciding to start medication. I went from having 1291 t cells and 9,100 copies of the virus in my system to having 685 t cells within a 6 month period. I have been on medications for six months and I am undetectable with 1260 t cells. The sex wasn't worth it. I wish I could change it.

Statistics

1. The National Gay and Lesbian Task Force's "National Anti-Gay/Lesbian Victimization Report": 45% of gay males and 20% of lesbians surveyed reported having experienced verbal harassment and or physical violence during high school as a result of their sexual orientation.

2. The Gay, Lesbian and Straight Education Network: 90% of LGBT youth reported that they sometimes or frequently heard homophobic comments in their schools.

3. U.S. Department of Health and Human Services: 20-40% of homeless youth in urban areas are homosexual.

4. The National Network of Runaway and Youth Services: 27% of homosexual teens moved away from home because of conflict with family members over sexual orientation.

5. Williams Institute's "Same-sex and Different sex couples in the American Community Survey 2005-2011": Same sex unions often have a higher household income.

6. National Gay and Lesbian Task Force (NGLTF): 20% of college students fear for their physical safety due to their gender identity or their perceived sexual orientation.

7. Williams Institute's "Same-sex and Different sex couples in the American Community Survey 2005-2011": 46% of same sex couples are more likely to have a degree.

8. Columbia University HIV Center for Clinical and Behavioral Studies: 68% of adolescent gay males use alcohol and 44% use other drugs; 83% of lesbians use alcohol and 56% use other drugs.

9. Centers for Disease Control and Prevention: Gay and bisexual men accounted for 69% new HIV infections in 2018. Of those diagnoses, 37% were Black or African American men, 30% were Hispanic/Latino men, and 27% were White men.

10. Top percentages of gay and lesbian parents in the United States: D.C. 28.6%, Massachusetts 16.4%, California 9.8%, New Mexico 9%, Alaska 8.6%.

Gone Too Soon

Like many homosexuals, 18-year-old Tyler Clementi felt rejected by his parents. After he went off to college, his roommate planted a camera in their common area and exposed Clementi for having a homosexual relationship. Tyler was found dead in the Hudson river. His last Facebook post was, "Jumping off the gw bridge sorry."
Tyler Clementi (December 19, 1991 – September 22, 2010)

Bullies

Sexual identity crises appear more frequently among teens and young adults. This creates a very sensitive period during junior high and high school years. As highlighted before, homosexual youth are five times more likely to attempt suicide than heterosexual youth. This is because the damages inflicted at such a vulnerable emotional stage can be catastrophic and follow someone for a lifetime. Bullying can take many forms. Physical intimidation, stealing, name calling, public shaming, and more.

Bullies wield ridicule: Spreading rumors and posting online names are a few common bullying techniques. Many LGBT teens have reported verbal harassment and physical assault on school grounds based on their sexual orientation and gender identity. They continue to note the lack of assistance from school officials. Some even contended that administrators inflicted public humiliation.

The best thing to do when getting bullied as a teen or adolescent is to tell both your parents and officials. Some believe this recourse makes them look weak or that this somehow will increase the attacks; however, the involvement of parents, teachers and, if necessary, law enforcement, is more likely to minimize or limit the amount of abuse. Parents and teachers should always report bullying as it may save a child's life. It's important for care-providers to encourage children to stick to groups of supportive friends and work on enjoyable extracurricular activities that may help build confidence. Bullied teens and young adults should be taught social awareness and how to avoid a situation, as well as assertiveness and how to stand his or her ground.

Celebrity Quote

"My feeling about gay people is that we have a responsibility not only to make gay marriage acceptable and to make gays feel accepted as much as heterosexuals…Gay people are downtrodden. They are beaten. They are abused for their sexuality, and it goes across race. In the White community and the Black community gay people are the bastards of the world. And in order for things to change, because any one of you could have gay children, or gay relatives, or gay friends…we have a responsibility to make this acceptable, to get all this bullsh-t so that some gay kid going to high school doesn't get the shit beaten out of him just because he's gay…I'm as heterosexual as they come. What is this hang-up about gay marriage? Who cares? Get on with your life!" **Howard Stern**

No situation is exactly the same, and there is no skeleton key that can open the door to emotional growth and intelligence. If bullying increases to a severe point, it is important to speak out. Tell as many people as you feel comfortable with. Someone will listen.

This could mean forming a GSA (Gay, Straight, Alliance) in your school or town. It could even mean contacting an already established group and opening lines of communication. Psychological help and counseling is out there for those who need it and may be provided for free by some non-profit companies.

The Trevor Lifeline at (866) 488-7386 is a free counseling center that specializes in the prevention of gay suicide.

LGBT Youth Centers in the United States

The Ali Forney Center
224 W. 35th St., 15th Floor, New York, NY
t: 212. 222.3427

ALSO Out Youth
1470 Blvd of the Arts, Sarasota, FL
t. 941. 951.2576

Attic Youth Center
255 S. 16th St., Philadelphia, PA
t. 215. 545.4331

Avenues for Youth
1708 Oak Park Ave, N. Minneapolis, MN
t. 612.522.1690

BAGLY
14 Beacon St., Floor 3, Boston, MA
t. 617.227.4313

The Billy DeFrank Center

938 The Alameda, San Jose, CA
t. 408.293.3040

Camp Lightbulb
Provincetown, MA
t. 508.237.7651

Center on Halsted
3656 N. Halsted St., Chicago, IL
t. 773.472.6469

Chris Kids
1017 Fayetteville Rd., Suite B, Atlanta, GA
t. 404.244.4156

The DC Center
2000 14th St. NW, Suite 105, Washington, DC
t. 202.682.2245

EmergencyYouth Shelter
1614 East Kane Place, Milwaukee, WI
t. 414.271.1560

Essex County RAIN Foundation
168 Park St., East Orange, NJ
t. 862.444.0582 or 732.707.RAIN (732.707.7246)

Gay & Lesbian Youth Services of Western NY
371 Delaware Ave, Buffalo, NY
t. 716.855.0221

GLBTAYS
2004 Poole Drive, NW Suites B & C, Huntsville, AL
t. 256.886.1150

Hatch Youth
401 Branard St., Houston, TX
t. 713.529.3211

Hetrick Martin Institute
2 Astor Place, Floor 3, New York, NY
t. 212.674.2400

Home O' Hope
Denver, CO
t. 303.442.3947

JASMYN
923 Peninsular Place, Jacksonville, FL
t. 904.389.3857

Just Us
Atlanta, GA
t. 470.399.2028

Life Ties
2205 Pennington Rd., Trenton, NJ
t. 609.771.1600

Lifeworks
1125 N. Mccadden Place, Los Angeles, CA
t. 323.860.7373

Lucie's Place
Little Rock, AR
t. 1.855.LuciesP (1.855.582.4377)

New Alternatives
83 Christopher St., New York, NY

Out Youth
909 E. 49 1/2 St., Austin, TX
t: 512.419.1233

Ozone House
1705 Washtenaw Ave, Ann Arbor, MI
t. 734.662.2222

Pathfinders
4200 North Holton St., Suite 400, Milwaukee, WI
t. 414.964.2565

Peter Cicchino Youth Project
40 Rector St., 9th Floor, New York, NY
t. 877.LGBT.LAW (877.542.8529)

Pridelines
9526 NE 2nd Ave, #104, Miami Shores, FL
t. 305.571.9601

Pride for Youth
2740 Martin Ave, Bellmore, NY
t. 516.826.0244

Project Fierce
751 N. Clark St., Chicago, IL
t. 812.236.8767

The Q Center (9 locations)
4115 N. Mississippi Ave, Portland, OR
t. 503.234.7837

The Q Spot
66 S. Main St., Suite B, Ocean Grove, NJ
t. 732. 455-3373

Ruth Ellis Center
616 E. Philadelphia St., Detroit, MI
t. 313.871.2145

Safe Spaces
4423 Lehigh Road, #192, College Park, MD
t. 240.776.2059

SMYAL
410 7th St., SE, Washington, DC

t. 202.546.5940

Stand Up For Kids
83 Walton St., Suite 300, Atlanta, GA
t. 1.800.365.4KID (1.800.365.4543)

Time OUT Youth
1900 The Plaza, Charlotte, NC
t. 704.344.8335

WAGLY
309 Washington St., Wellesley Hills, MA
t. 508.875.2122

The YEAH! Program
Berkley, CA
t. 888.456.7890

Youth Care
5825 16th Ave, NE Seattle, WA
t. 206.522.8412

Youth First Texas
3918 Harry Hines Blvd, Dallas, TX
t. 214.879.0400

The Waltham House – 110 Pond St., Waltham, MA
t. 781.894.3319

Zebra Youth – 911 North Mills Ave, Orlando, FL
t. 877.909.3272

Anonymous Artist
How did I know?

It was during the summer of 2007. I was still in school. I was what you call the popular kid that everyone wanted to hate on because of a girl. I walked the halls of the school with confidence, never worried about what people said. I didn't start drama, didn't too much like it. I had a lot of friends. Most of us played ball for the school that season. We were bad too; no one could stop us.

We had just got done play[ing] four quarters and going into two overtimes. It was about the best game all season. Everyone did their job and did it well. When the game was over we hung our heads in victory. Everyone came to the middle of the court to celebrate with the team. It was the first trip for our school to the state games in 23 years.

After all the victory celebrations, dancing, taking pictures, giving hugs and signing autographs. After all that we could finally hit the showers and get ready to go home. Me and my best friend were the last to enter the showers because we had an interview with the local new broadcasting team. As we got out of our jersey's I felt a great feeling of attraction towards him. I don't know where it came from, but like seeing him strip in front of me this time just made me hard. Trying to hide it I quickly turned to the other side of the bench, and continued the conversation.

As hard as I tried to hide that something was wrong with me, I'm afraid that he knew me too well. He then walked up behind me tapping on my shoulders trying to figure out what was the matter with me. Every question he asked my knees got weaker and weaker, and I got harder and harder. After about ten minutes of questioning he walked toward the shower, he turned around and asked was I going to join him. My answer, "yea give me a minute, cuz." "iight," he replied.

> As I walked in the shower room, I saw the water dripping down all the right areas of his body. I took myself to a corner, and turned the water on. We had a good convo going on about the game. How he felt that he out did me on the floor "yea right" I thought to myself. I finally got comfortable with the conversation, so I turned to face him. A few minutes after I turned around to talk face to face, he had a very different look on his face. A more serious look. A look like something was about to go down. To my surprise he asked me, "Can I ask you a question on the real?" I said, "Yea show kid"
>
> Then to my surprise he asked, "Have you ever looked at me in a different way?" "What?" I responded.
>
> "Like have you ever wanted to fuck feel me inside of you, anything like that." Let me remind you this is my one and only best friend, I can't lie I replied "yea all the time." Not knowing what the outcome of my response would be. He then said "cool, me too."
>
> Getting deeper and deeper into the conversation we started hugging, rubbing, kissing and laughing. I then asked if he could put himself inside me, just to see how it felt. He said "yes, but I needed a condom." He told me to grab one out of his locker. He put it on "boy you know I think about you day and night."

Internalized Homophobia

Psychiatrists have drawn links between homophobia and homosexual desire. Studies related that people with stronger homophobic gravitations have shown to have suppressed homosexual urges. Internalized homophobia occurs when a homosexual hates themselves based on their sexuality. Said to cause depression, substance abuse issues, and dangerous sexual behaviors, some form is reported to be in most homosexuals. As geography holds some responsibility, upbringing has a lot to do with the formation of self-hating persons. Religion, family viewpoints, and damaging stereotypes have all caused those with internalized homophobia to embody shame and sometimes even hurt themselves because of their existence.

"Homophobia is weird.
There's no real competition between gay and straight men. More girls for the heteros...is that really a Problem?"

Links to Homophobia and Homosexuality

In 1996, the University of Georgia compared homophobia to homosexual arousal. They brought together two groups of men who indentified as straight—35 homophobic men and 29 non-homophobic men—and measured their arousal using penile plethysmography. Both groups were shown erotic videotapes of hetero and homosexual nature. Both groups tested similarly when it came to viewing heterosexual and lesbian videos, but when shown videos of homosexual men, the results varied: 54% of homophobic men showed significant arousal compared to 24% of non-homophobic men.[42]

Anonymous Artist

The girl stick in between ! I know how it feels
To look in mirror
Wish
There was pill
Boy
Girl
Ying, yang
Isn't the soul made up of masculine/ feminine energy
So I write these words
To say I will no longer be stuck I choose life

> If need be
> I choose the knife
> If u could see my soul
> Written
> All over
> Would be
> Woman, girl, lady....
> In pink hues
> I'm a girl choosing
> Not someone losing
> My mind is free
> Now my body can breathe

"Sometimes people are threatened by gays and lesbians because they are fearing their own impulses, in a sense they 'doth protest too much,'" described Richard Ryan, a professor of psychology at the University of Rochester. "In addition, it appears that sometimes those who would oppress others have been oppressed themselves, and we can have some compassion for them too; they may be unaccepting of others because they cannot be accepting of themselves."

History has painted femininity as weak. Seen in men, these qualities can be viewed as funny or shameful. It is important to realize the difference between flamboyance and annoyance. Limiting oneself to gay stereotypes can be just as bad as ostracizing them. Dealing with internalized homophobia can be a struggle, but as in most battles, knowledge plays an intricate role in overcoming.

"Educate yourself and find the beauty in your differences! You might find power in being Unique!

Chapter 6

Mainstream Gayness

Growing up, it is common to look for role models. Any child regardless of race or creed observes the world around them to find their place in society. Subconsciously, we learn who we are through watching others. We relate with those who share like characteristics and model ourselves after what we see. But we have no control as to what is shown to us.

With regard to race, Eleni Delimaltadaki Janis, public opinion and media research coordinator for the Opportunity Agenda in New York, reports, "When media producers in journalism and popular culture media like movies, television series and video games are mostly White, chances that young people will be humanized and fully represented are slim."

She goes on to say, "You see few images of Black men and boys being good students or being good fathers. They're really fewer images of men in those roles compared to reality. It's not just the news coverage. It's also every type of media, but also in entertainment media, including video games. They all do a good job at using negative images of Black boys and men for entertainment."[43]

When certain images are instilled at a young age, the unhealthy result is ambition limited to stereotypical and social standards. For some it is easier to fall into a slightly relatable stereotype than it is to understand one's uniqueness and ability to succeed. Homosexuals are not limited to occupations in fashion or design and, like all sects of people, possess a cornucopia of important skill sets. Just as when the media depicts race in a shadowed light, individuals must not base their sexual identities on society's stereotypes.

What the media has to say about homosexuality

Media's portrayal of homosexuality has varied. Because of politics and social aggressions, homosexuality has been seen in a more favored light in the more recent years, however common stereotypes are often showcased. Gay men are seen as overly flamboyant, bold, and promiscuous.

Upholding cliches such as these only promote homophobia and poison gay youth with limiting outlooks on self-worth. In fact, it is a popular belief that gays should be removed from all children's entertainment. For example, when Ellen DeGeneres came out of the closet in 1997, sponsors such as the fast food establishment Wendy's, pulled their advertisements.

LGBT people are still highly distorted in the media. Progressive television shows such as *Will and Grace* and *Modern Family* commented on gay stereotypes but still told the sugar coated stories of rich, gay White men and rarely dealt with extinguishing gay myths, especially within the minority community. Television series like *Orange is the New Black* have brought transgender characters into mainstream, including Laverne Cox's role as Sophia Burset, but have failed to spotlight LGBT issues as a whole.

Gay Stereotypes Often Portrayed In The Media

1. Having a lisp or a limp wrist is often a stereotype associated with gay individuals.

SERIOUSLY. There is no scientific connection between having a limp wrist and being homosexual.

2. Gays are more promiscuous and sexually careless than heterosexual people.

SERIOUSLY. While the common retort is that men tend to be more sexual than women in general, everyone one gets down, and anyone can engage in high risk sexual activity.

3. Bisexual men just can't admit they're gay.

SERIOUSLY. Sexuality is fluid and desires of a particular gender increase and decrease over time.

4. Gays do nothing but party and consume drugs.

SERIOUSLY. Though it has been proven that due to external factors gay youth are more likely to experiment with drugs, it is certainly not the defining law to being a homosexual. Statistically, gay males are less likely to go to college, yet they are also more likely to receive a degree.

Contributions by Gays to Society

Alan Mathison Turing (1912 – 1954) Considered the British father of artificial intelligence, this computer scientist has changed the world with his model for the home computer. The 2014 historical drama *The Imitation Game* depicts Turing's code-breaking genius, which secured British victory in WWII, as well as his gut-wrenching punishment of chemical castration.

Barbara Gittings (1961-2007) Credited for the movement to change the psychiatric/psycholohical profession view on homesexuality as a mental pathology.

Barney Frank (1940)the Massachusetts House Representative who introduced the anti discrimination ban in housing, employment, and public accommodations.

Bayard Rustin (1912-1987) Chief organizer of the 1963 March on Washington where Rev. Martin Luther King Jr. delivered his famous speech, "I Have a Dream"

Gus Van Sant (1952) Film director, screenwriter, musician and author. Sant directed such Best Picture Nominations as *Good Willing Hunting* (1997) and *Milk* (2008) and has also been nominated twice for the Academy Award for Best Director.

Harry Hay (1912-2002) Started the Gay Liberation Front.

Harvey Milk (1930-1978)One of America's first openly gay elected officials. He is responsible for the gay liberation movement before his assassination.

James Baldwin (1924-1987) American novelist, playwrite, essayist, poet, and activist.

Katharine Lee Bates (1859 – 1929) American poet and songwriter. Author of "America the Beautiful," "America the Dream" and "The Story of Chaucer's Canterbury Pilgrims."

Leonardo Da Vinci (1452-1519) Renaissance man of art, engineering, and science. He designed the first sketches of a helicopter years before the Wright Brothers.

Malcolm Stevenson Forbes (1919 – 1990) Publisher of *Forbes* magazine.

Robert Baden-Powell (1857 – 1941) British army veteran who founded the Boy Scouts.

Sally Ride (1951-2012) America's First female astronaut

Sophie Wilson (1957) Transgender British computer scientist who designed the Acorn Micro-Computers.

Thomas Lanier "Tennessee" Williams (1911 – 1983) American playwright and author of *A Streetcar Named Desire*, *Sweet Bird of Youth*, and *Cat on a Hot Tin Roof*.

Truman Capote (1924 – 1984) Outspoken author of *In Cold Blood*.

Willem Arondeus (1894-1943) A member of the anti-Nazi resistance movement in World War II and planned the 1943 bombing of the Amsterdam civil registry office which saved many Jews from arrest and deportation to the extermination camps. He was caught and executed after exclaiming, "Tell the people that homosexuals can be brave!"

Gay Slang

Bareback: unprotected sex

Bear: a large, hairy man

Bi-curious: a person who does not identify has bisexual but has a desire to explore

Blow job: oral sex

Bottom: receptive sexual partner

Breeder: derogatory term for heterosexuals

Butch: masculine lesbian

Civil Union: an agreement that allows gay some benefits of marriage but not all

Closeted: someone who refused to admit homosexual tendencies

Coming out: admitting to the world their homosexuality

Cross-dresser: a straight or gay man or woman who sometimes dresses in the clothes of the opposite gender

Cub: a younger bear

Daddy: older, financially established gay man

Discreet or DL: gay man who keeps a secretive identity

Drag Queen: a gay man that portrays a separate often over dramatized female character

Fag: perviously defining a cigarette or a bundle of sticks now is a derogatory name for a gay man

Fag Hag: female best friend to a gay male

Femme: possessing more feminine qualities

Feathered: polished and glamours

Fierce: fearless and beautiful

Fishy: showing female qualities

Flaming: overly gay

Fox: slender, slightly fit and attractive young looking male

F2M: female transiting to male

Gold Star: a person who has only exhibited homosexual relations

Gym Bunny/Muscle Mary: a fit homosexual

Hasbian: a woman who perviously identified as a lesbian

Jock: athletic gay male

Kiki: a social gathering where gossip is exchanged

Lipstick Lesbian: a more feminized lesbian

M2F: male transitioning to female

Otter: thinner, hairier gay men

Poz: HIV positive person

Queen: feminine man

Raw: unprotected sex

Tea: gossip

Trade: a masculine and secretive gay man

Tranny: a controversial word referring to transgender people

Top: penetrating sexual partner

Twink: young-looking effeminate man

Verse: Someone who enjoys both bottom and top positions

Wolf: a man that falls between a twin and a bear

Yaz/Yes: a general sign of approval

Celebrity Quote
"I didn't know I was a gay icon. I get a lot of mail—but I don't get many bad letters—but I got a woman the other day that was so upset with me because they said, 'How do you feel about the gay marriage thing?' and my answer to that is, 'I really don't care with whom you sleep, I just care what kind of a decent human being you are.' I figure all the rest of it is your business and not mine. And not hers, incidentally." **Betty White**

Just a Few Gay Icons

A gay icon is a figure in the media who is readily embraced and accepted by the gay community. As role models, they often display bravery, glamour, femininity, strength, and sometimes androgyny. These idols have represented a pool of resilience because they are known to stand up against gender norms and exemplify societal overcoming.

Anderson Cooper (1967) An out American journalist and author, he is an Emmy award winner and hosted his own talk show.

"The fact is, I'm gay, always have been, always will be, and I couldn't be any more happy, comfortable with myself, and proud."

Angelina Jolie (1975) World famous actor and producer, she has also made political history.

"I've realized that being happy is a choice. You never want to rub anybody the wrong way or not be fun to be around, but you have to be happy. When I get logical and I don't trust my instincts—that's when I get in trouble."

Bette Midler (1945) Broadway star, singer, actress, and all around diva, she got her start performing in bathhouses and has since become a gay idol and star. In 2016, she openly supported the *Hamilton* audience's reception of Vice President Pence: "Anyone who says 'yay' to gay conversion DESERVES to be booed at a Broadway musical."

"Despite the way things turned out [with the AIDS crisis], I'm still proud of those days. I feel like I was at the forefront of the gay liberation movement, and I hope I did my part to help move it forward. So, I kind of wear the label of 'Bathhouse Betty' with pride."

Beyoncé Knowles (1981) Accomplished singer famous for her feminist views, she has been embraced by the gay community and is a drag queen favorite.

"If you like it you should be able to put a ring on it. We will unite for marriage equality!"

Britney Spears (1981) Known for her sexually unapologetic music, she has gained a large fan base, especially within the gay community.

"A lot of my hair stylists and my beauty team that I work with are gay so I hang out with gays a lot and I just think they're adorable and hilarious."

Celine Dion (1968) Beloved Canadian singer Celine Dion has supported the gay community and stated in regards to her child:

"If he's a gay person, he's not any less of my son."

Cher (1946) Legendary holder of the GLAAD Media Award, Cher represents strength and power within the gay community.

"Is this true? Marcus Bachmann has a Christian clinic where he de-programs gay boys and girls! I'm gonna strangle him with my Boa!"

Clay Aiken (1978) American singer who gained his fame during the second season of *American Idol*, Aiken has spoken out for gay rights in several campaigns and has even ran for political office.

"To imply that, as a gay man, I have to speak to gay issues only, or more than anything else, would be the same as implying that a Jewish candidate should only speak up for Jewish constituents, or that a Black candidate should only speak up for Black constituents."

Coretta Scott King (1927 – 2006) Wife of Martin Luther King Jr., Coretta has shown her support for gay rights throughout her life. By comparing the LGBT struggle to the civil rights movement she made history by allowing room for lesbian speakers, despite homophobic tensions, during rallies and debates.

"Homophobia is like racism and anti-Semitism and other forms of bigotry in that it seeks to dehumanize a large group of people, to deny their humanity, their dignity and personhood. This sets the stage for further repression and violence that spread all too easily to victimize the next minority group."

Ellen DeGeneres (1958) Television host, actress, comedian, and writer, Ellen has historically opened a path for artists behind her as she bravely came out on her talk show and became a spokesperson for the gay community:

"I think they should have a Barbie with a buzz cut."

Elton John (1947) Out and accredited British singer, songwriter, and composer, Elton has gotten involved with many gay issues and vowed to raise gay rights.

"I know a lot of people, and perhaps especially religious people, will say that David and I should count ourselves lucky for living in a country that allows civil partnerships, and call it quits there… Well, I don't accept this. I don't accept it because there is a world of difference between calling someone your 'partner' and calling them your 'husband.' 'Partner' is a word that should be preserved for people you play tennis with, or work alongside in business. It doesn't come close to describing the love that I have for David, and he for me. In contrast, 'husband' does. A 'husband' is somebody that you cherish forever, that you would give up everything for, that you love in sickness and in health. Until the law recognizes David Furnish is my husband, and not merely my partner, the law won't describe the man I know and adore.... Wouldn't it be a huge source of national pride if we led, rather than just followed, the currents of history, and became one of the first countries in the world to say being married isn't about whether you're straight or gay, but about whether you're human?"

Harvey Milk (1930 – 1978) First openly gay politician to hold an elected office in the history of California.

"Burst down those closet doors once and for all, and stand up and start to fight."

Janet Jackson (1948) Janet has spoken out against homophobia and supported gay love ever since she gained her strong homosexual following in the '90s.

"I don't mind people thinking that I'm gay or calling me gay. People are going to believe whatever they want. Yes, I hang out at gay clubs, but other clubs too. I go where the music is good. I love people regardless of sexual preference, regardless of race. No, I am not bisexual. I have been linked with dancers in our group because we are so close. I grew up in a big family. I love being affectionate. I love intimacy and I am not afraid to show it. We fall asleep in each other's arms. We hug, we kiss, but there is nothing beyond that. Because [René Elizondo, Jr.] and I broke up, it's like people need some sort of drama, some sort of gossip."

Johnny Weir (1984) Weir is an out American olympic figure skater and owner of the 2008 bronze. He also created the Johnny & Victor Weir-Voronov Scholarship Fund for LGBTQ Youth.

"No mother wants to hear her son say he's gay. Those two words rip the picture of a daughter-in- law and grandchildren into pieces. I felt sorry for my mom and wanted her to know everything was going to be all right. But then she said, 'I don't really care, Johnny, as long as I know that you are going to be happy.'"

Joan Rivers (1933 – 2014) Comedian, historic talk show host, and gay rights advocate.

"I HATE gay weddings. I'm thrilled about the equal rights thing ... but gay weddings are like the War on Terror—they go on forever.... Gay weddings are a lifetime commitment—for the guests. They start at seven and end in October. Why? Because stereotypes be damned, gays love parades."

Kathy Griffin (1960) Long-time supporter of gay rights, outspoken comedian Griffin has hosted many gay events and stressed the importance of equal rights regardless of sex.

"I started doing the gay clubs and getting a better response. I find that gay audiences are more raucous, somewhat political and knowledgable."

Kylie Minogue (1968) A pop star who considers herself "adopted by the gay community" has headlined the Sydney Gay and Lesbian Mardi Gras.

"I didn't become a gay icon or become popular in the gay community for doing something specific. That happened just because I was being myself."

Lady Gaga (1986) Stefani Joanne Angelina Germanotta is an American singer and songwriter who has aligned herself with the gay community since her debut. Gaga has made her mark by commenting in favor of several gay issues and has even supported her love to the gay community through her musical lyrics.

"I just want to be clear before we decide to do this together: I'm gay. My music is gay. My show is gay. And I love that it's gay. And I love my gay fans and they're all going to be coming to our show. And it's going to remain gay."

Anonymous Artist
First Time

Make sure the mood is right and that this is what you really want to do... Cleanliness is next to godliness...so make sure you're prepared in that way...a good "fleet" douche followed by a warm water douche until the water you excrete is clean. Also make sure that you have expelled all water from your rectum...your friend should know and expect there might be some "paint" given this is your first time...if that happens don't be embarrassed, just clean up and go from there...my advice is to use plenty of lube. He should also be a gentleman and take it easy.

If it hurts tell him. If it's too painful don't let him continue. He should understand that as well. I also suggest that you be on top (riding) that way you're more in control of what's going on. Just remember to relax!

Whatever position you choose; easy does it. A little bit at a time. Don't let him just dog you out! Make sure that you're respected in the end and enjoy. Your first time can be [a] great experience or a nightmare...!! Remember you call the shots. If you tell him to stop. That's what you mean, don't feel pressured.

Laverne Cox (1934) First transgender advocate to be nominated for an Emmy, Cox has produced shows and has been the first transgender person to cover *Time* magazine.

"When I saw *Boys Don't Cry*, I was trying to decide if I wanted to transition or not. I remember seeing Brandon Teena killed and I thought, 'Oh, my God, I'm going to die.'"

Madonna (1958) Singer and songwriter who has pushed many boundaries and gained a large homosexual fan base for her support and bravery.

"You cannot use the name of God or religion to justify acts of violence to hurt, to hate, to discriminate."

Mariah Carey (1970) Supporter of gay rights, Carey has insisted her music is for anyone that feels different.

"Just keep believing!—I know that's cliché, and it would be typical of me to say something like that. It's almost impossible to say anything, really, except you must be aware that dealing with that in high school is a passing place. You have to stay strong, rely on your true friends, and try to get through it, as opposed to drowning in it. Look at how many people suffered during high school and came out of it a better, stronger adult. That's the thing to focus on."

Michael Sam (1990) First out gay player to be drafted into the NFL.

"I knew from a young age that I was attracted to guys. Growing up, I didn't know if it was a phase. I wanted to find who I was—I wanted to make sure to find who I am. Now that I know I am gay, I am comfortable in my skin."

Neil Patrick Harris (1973) Out actor who has won a Tony and four Emmys. Harris and his long-time husband David Burtka are an inspiring celebrity couple who publicly announced their engagement in 2011 when New York passed the Marriage Equality Act.

"Being able to live my life transparently does empower me to feel like I can be myself more. It's easier for me to flirt with girls now that girls know that I'm gay. It almost makes it a sexier encounter than if I was trying to pretend that I was straight."

Oprah Winfrey (1954) Considered one of the most powerful women in the world, Oprah has fought for equality and battled LGBT issues on her talk show.

"I've never had a straight couple come to me and say, 'My marriage is in trouble because of a gay couple living next door.'"

Rosie O'Donnell (1962) A comedian, actress and out LGBT rights activist. In 2002, Rosie made headlines when she came out and spearheaded adoption rights for gay parents.

"I'm not asking that people accept homosexuality. I'm not asking that they believe like I do that it's inborn. I'm not asking that. All I'm saying is don't let these children suffer without a family because of your bias."

Rupaul (1960) Internationally famous drag queen and actor, Rupal has changed the world's views on sexuality.

"If you don't love yourself, how in the hell you gonna love somebody else?"

Zachary Quinto (1977) Actor and film producer who came out of the closet in 2011 after the suicide of gay teenager Jamey Rodemeyer. He is quoted:

"Living a gay life without publicly acknowledging it is simply not enough to make any significant contribution to the immense work that lies ahead on the road to complete equality."

Popular Gay Movies/ Documentaries

Paris is Burning (1990) is an historical documentary which took a glimpse into urban gay and transgender communities. The film served as a raw account of American social views on homosexuality at the time.

The Crying Game (1992) is a dangerous British thriller which tackles gender, race, and identity issues.

Philadelphia (1993), starring Tom Hanks, provides a poignant portrayal of an HIV positive lawyer facing discrimination and homophobia in the 1980s. The film kicked down mainstream doors as the first Hollywood hit to showcase AIDS and homosexuality.

The Adventures of Priscilla, Queen of the Desert (1994) is a comedy that joins a bunch of drag queens on their road trip full of misadventures.

To Wong Foo, Thanks for Everything! Julie Newmar (1995) is a cult classic comedy that portrays the bonds of friendship between three drag queens.

Beautiful Thing (1996) tells the story of two men who meet through a violence encounter but discover love through strange circumstances.

The Birdcage (1996) features an iconic performance from Robin Williams in this sassy remake, which won the SAG Award for Outstanding Performance by a Cast in a Motion Picture.

The Rocky Horror Picture Show (1975) is a cult classic horror musical that became a symbol of gay rights with its crossdressing star (Tim Curry) and over the top celebration of sexual liberation.

Boys Don't Cry (1999), winner of best film of the year, is a retelling of real life transgender man Brandon Teena and the tragedy he underwent to find love.

Trick (1999) is a fun romantic comedy that glorifies one night stands through sexual misadventures and friendships.

But I'm a Cheerleader (2000) is an indie film that finds a former cheerleader sent to a gay conversion boot camp. The film is known for its controversial depiction of female masturbation and pleasure.

Hedwig and the Angry Inch (2001) is cult classic musical comedy based around a genderqueer rockstar's search for fame and love.

Brokeback Mountain (2005), an adaptation of Annie Proulx's short story, features the epic love tale of two men in the American West. Nominated for eight Academy Awards and winner of three, this film challenged the social constructs of masculinity.

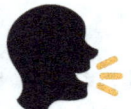

**Anonymous Artist
How did you come out?**

I came out to my parents when I was young. I can't remember if it was in the eighth or ninth grade though. I consider myself bisexual, but the fact that I was attracted to boys really bothered me because I knew it was "wrong". That's what I was taught at the time by the church. The only people who knew before my parents were my friends in school and my girlfriend at the time. I had also told my lesbian aunt because I needed some advice and moral support. I distinctly remember my best friend being so happy that she had a "gay" friend and she took it really well.

> Anyway, when I told my mother she broke down into tears which made me cry. She took it really hard at first. She called my dad over to the house so I could tell him. My dad saw that we were both crying and he was so concerned because he thought somebody had died. Once I finally told him, he took it so well. He literally said, "Wait, that's all? Y'all got me over here thinkin' somebody done died!" He went on to say that he didn't care who I ended up with, as long as I was happy and lived a good life.
>
> My dad just recently passed away this past November from lung cancer, but he has always been supportive of me and what I've done with my life. He was always proud of me for being a straight A student and going to college since I was the only one of his kids to ever go so that was his main concern. I remember that being strange because I always had thought that it would be my dad who wouldn't understand and my mother who'd be nurturing, but it was the other way around. My mother eventually came around and to this day she always says that she loves me no matter what.
>
> I think that there's still a little unease and hoping I marry a woman which may or may not happen, but when it is all said and done she loves me and just wants me to be happy. My mother and I have the best relationship ever.

Milk (2008), a biographical film based on the life of openly gay politician Harvey Milk, depicts Milk's short term in office and eventual assassination.

Shelter (2007), winner of the "Outstanding Film-Limited Release" at the 2009 GLAAD Media Awards, follows two male lovers who struggle against the odds.

G. B. F (Gay Best Friend) (2013) is an independent teen comedy exploring the highs and lows of social stigma that goes along with being gay.

Blue is the Warmest Color (2013) is a controversial international film that explores the sensual coming of age of its 15-year-old protagonist and her older, lesbian lover.

Boy Meets Girl (2015) brings the tender coming-of-age romance between a young transgender woman living in rural Virginia and her BFF to the fore in this sex positive film.

Moonlight (2016) is the first LGBT movie to win an Academy Award for Best Picture. This coming-of-age drama tells the story of a young Black man growing up in Miami and is based on the play *In Moonlight Black Boys Look Blue*.

Love, Simon (2018), based on the novel *Simon vs. the Homo Sapiens*, takes an upbeat and heartfelt approach to coming out of the closet and finding one's identity while navigating high school.

The Boys in the Band (2020), based on the groundbreaking 1968 play of the same name, features dynamic characters played by 9 out and proud leading gay men. The film uses comedy to explore the historical journey of gay life in the public image.

Chapter 7

Am I gay?

Well, are you?

You don't have to answer that right now. Believe it or not, most people ask themselves this question at some point in their lives. Others can ask themselves this all of their lives and still never come up with a clear answer. It is natural for many heterosexual men to sometimes have male fantasies, or even get aroused through male interaction. This does not prove homosexuality, bisexuality, or even bi-curiousness. The truth is, no one can decide your sexuality, not even you. You can choose whether to act on it, but denying urges or thoughts could be detrimental. A great place to start is by asking if you have both emotional and physical attractions to the same sex.

Honesty and bravery are key when answering this question. Being a happy person, in general, requires sacrifice. When disputing your sexuality, you must give up caring what others may think. This fear has crippled many homosexuals as many people find it hard to admit to others their sexuality and live in denial. It is not a small feat to overcome, but finding the strength to be yourself, regardless of what family or society may think, is true courage.

Another sacrifice to be made is straight privilege. Let's face it, it isn't easy to actively choose a life you know could be problematic for you. Straight privileges include relationship support, community bonding, and looser employment standards. Even small things—such as Him and Her bath towels or popular music only representing straight couples—can make you feel like you don't belong. The world as we know it caters to a certain group of people, and living outside of that group can be lonely and scary. Renouncing straight privilege can be one of the most difficult steps in the coming out process. Many tend to force themselves into boxes not realizing the benefits from creating a box of your own.

Saving your body until you're ready can be a great way to get to know yourself; alternatively, some choose to step out of their comfort zone and experiment. Whichever way you decide to get to know yourself, it is just important that you start. Knowing yourself, regardless of how you identify, is the first step to loving and respecting the real you.

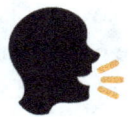

Celebrity Quote
"It's a no-brainer. If you're not for gay marriage, don't marry a gay person." **Whoopi Goldberg**

Safe Sex

If you do choose to experiment, it is vital to practice safe sex. Because of the shameful reputation of homosexuality, gay sex has been shrouded in mystery and for some, can only be explored in secret and dangerous settings. These seedy interactions further promote stereotypes but are most importantly unsafe and can be life threatening. As previously mentioned, the Centers for Disease Control and Prevention recorded that 69% of new HIV infections are reported in gay and bisexual men. The study has shown that approximately a third of the infected have no idea. Homophobia and stigma may deter some from getting tested or reaching for high-quality services. However, in order to not be treated like a second-class citizen you have to hold your body and your safety in high esteem.

"No matter how cute he is, it is YOUR responsibility to remain safe and to know your status! Trust me, all it takes in one time and no matter how good it is, it isn't worth your life."

How to come out

If you choose to acknowledge your homosexuality, then next step is to eventually **come out of the closet**. There is no clear cut way to come out: We are individuals with our own unique situations and obstacles. Safety, as always, comes first. If you are in a position where you fear physical danger, remove yourself from the situation before you come out. If you do not fear physical attacks, then prepare yourself for verbal ones. More than often, shock can burst into other emotions. Phobias are hard to overcome and perceived notions may require some time and education to fix. No one is perfect, and the reaction that you get may not be the one you need.

"Coming out isn't easy, but most people are happier once they do!"

It helps to first tell people who you know you'll get a positive response from. Usually a close relative or friend may understand. If there is no one in your life you feel like you can go to, try writing it down and familiarizing yourself with your newfound fact. You are allowed to come out in small doses if this makes you more comfortable. However, the most important thing to remember is to love yourself and be proud of who you are.

References

(1) Fereydooni, Arash. "Do Animals Exhibit Homosexuality?" Yale Scientific Magazine. Yale University, Mar.-Apr. 2012. Web. 20 Jan. 2015. https://www.yalescientific.org/2012/03/do-animals-exhibit-homosexuality/

Mooallem, Jon. "Can Animals Be Gay?" The New York Times. The New York Times, 03 Apr. 2010. Web. 20 Jan. 2015. http://www.nytimes.com/2010/04/04/magazine/ 04animals-t.html

(2) Schwartz, John. "Of Gay Sheep, Modern Science and Bad Publicity." The New York Times. The New York Times, 24 Jan. 2007. Web. 20 Jan. 2015. http://www.nytimes.com/2007/01/25/science/25sheep.html

(3) Moskowitz, By Clara. "Same Sex Couples Common in the Wild." LiveScience. TechMedia Network, 16 May 2008. Web. 20 Jan. 2015. http://www.livescience.com/2534-sex-couples-common-wild.html

(4) Roughgarden, Joan. Evolution's Rainbow: Diversity, Gender, and Sexuality in Nature and People. Berkeley: U of California, 2004.

(5) Bem, D. J. (2008). Is there a causal link between childhood gender nonconformity and adult homosexuality? Journal of Gay & Lesbian Mental Health, 12, 61-79. http://www.dbem.ws/Exotic %20Becomes%20Erotic.pdf

(6) Levay, S. 1991. A Difference in Hypothalamic Structure between Heterosexual and Homosexual Men, Science 253:1034-1037. http://www.bu.edu/thenerve/ archives/spring-2010/reviews-spring-2010/homosexuality/ http://www.nerve.com/love-sex/the-science-of-sex-the-gay-brain-revisited

(7) Roselli CE, Larkin K, Resko JA, Stellflug JN, Stormshak F. 2004. The volume of a sexually dimorphic nucleus in the ovine medial preoptic area/anterior hypothalamus varies with sexual partner preference. Endocrinology 145:478-483 http://www.bu.edu/thenerve/archives/spring-2010/reviews-spring-2010/homosexuality/

http://press.endocrine.org/doi/abs/ 10.1210/en.2003-1098

(8) Roselli, Charles E., Kay Larkin, John A. Resko, John N. Stellflug, and Fred Stormshak. "The Volume of a Sexually Dimorphic Nucleus in the Ovine Medial Preoptic Area/Anterior Hypothalamus Varies with Sexual Partner Preference." : Endocrinology: Vol 145, No 2. Endocrine Science, July-Aug. 2013. http://press.endocrine.org/doi/abs/10.1210/en.2003-1098

(9) Allen LS, Gorski RA. 1992. Sexual orientation and size of the anterior commissure in the human brain, Proc Natl Acad Sci USA 89:7199–7202 https://www.ncbi.nlm.nih.gov/pmc/articles/PMC49673/

(10) 02, August. "Study Finds Structural Differences in Brains of Straight, Homosexual Men." Los Angeles Times. Los Angeles Times, 02 Aug. 1992. http://articles.latimes.com/1992-08-02/news/ mn-5715_1_brain-structure

(11) Ivanka Savic and Per Lindström. PET and MRI show differences in cerebral asymmetry and functional connectivity between homo- and heterosexual subjects. Proceedings of the National Academy of Sciences, 2008; http://www.sciencedaily.com/releases/ 2008/06/080617151845.htm

(12) "The Kinsey Institute - Kinsey Sexuality Rating Scale." The Kinsey Institute - Kinsey Sexuality Rating Scale. http://www.kinseyinstitute.org/research/ak-hhscale.html

(13) "The Klein Grid." http://www.americaninstituteofbisexuality.org/thekleingrid/

(14) "Young Southampton." Storms Sexuality Axis http:// https://sid.southampton.gov.uk/kb5/southampton/directory/advice.page?id=qzlkp5NvReI

(15) Murray, Stephen O. Homosexualities. N.p.: U of Chicago, n.d. Print.

(16) Laws on Homosexuality in African Nations. http://www.loc.gov/law/help/criminal-laws-on-homosexuality/laws-on-homosexuality-in-african-nations.pdf

(17) Orgbon, Charles. "Two-Spirit People: Gays Accepted by Native Americans." The Huffington Post. TheHuffingtonPost.com, http://www.huffingtonpost.com/charles-orgbon/twospirit-people-gays-acc_b_1677851.html

(18) Giago, Tim. "Native Americans and Homosexuality." The Huffington Post. TheHuffingtonPost.com http://www.huffingtonpost.com/tim-giago/native-americans-and-homosexuality_b_2267967.html

"Native American Netroots." Native American Netroots. http://nativeamericannetroots.net/diary/313

http://crl.ucsd.edu/~elman/Courses/HDP1/2000/ LectureNotes/williams.pdf

(19) "Employment of Homosexuals and Other Sex Perverts in Governement (1950)." PBS.

http://www.geni.com/people/James-E-Webb-2nd-Administrator-of-NASA/600000002214795324

(20) Wright, Lionel. "The Stonewall Riots – 1969." Socialist Alternative. N.p., 07 June 2014. http://www.socialistalternative.org/stonewall-riots-1969/

(21) "Stonewall Riots | United States History." Encyclopedia Britannica Online. Encyclopedia Britannica, http://www.britannica.com/EBchecked/topic/1386501/Stonewall-riots

(22) Editorial Board, World History of Male Love, "Homosexual Traditions," Chinese Tradition of Male Love, 2000 <http://www.gay-art-history.org/gay-history/gay-customs/china-gay-cut-sleeve/china-homosexual-bitten-peach.html>

(23) Lau, Steffi. "Homosexuality in China同性恋在 中国." US-China Today: Homosexuality in China.https://uschinatoday.org/features/2010/03/10/homosexuality-in-china/

(24) Star, Shanghai. "History of Chinese Homosexuality." https://www.chinadaily.com.cn/english/doc/2004-04/01/content_319807.htm

(25) Watanabe, Tsuneo. Love of the Samurai : A Thousand Years of Japanese Homosexuality. London: Gay Man's, 1989. Print. http://www.samurai-weapons.net/samurai-history/wakashudo-as-a-form-of-homosexuality-in-old- japan

(26) "1932 in LGBT Rights History | Timeline |." 1932 in LGBT Rights History | Timeline | Equaldex, The LGBT Knowledge Base. Equaldex, The LGBT Knowledge Base

(27) "Global LGBT Rights Advocate Calls for Day of "calling in Gay" to Work." Global LGBT Rights Advocate Calls for Day of "calling in Gay" to Work. http://www.prlog.org/12049819-global-lgbt-rights-advocate-calls-for-day-of-calling-in-gay-to- work.html

(28) Townley, Ben. "Saudi Arabia Arrests 110 Gay Men." Sodomy Laws. http://www.prlog.org/ 12049819-global-lgbt-rights-advocate-calls-for-day-of-calling-in-gay-to-work.html

(29) "Homosexuality and Buddhism." - ReligionFacts. http://www.religionfacts.com/ homosexuality/buddhism.ht

(30) Lattin, Don. "Dalai Lama Speaks on Gay Sex." SFGate. http://www.sfgate.com/news/article/Dalai-Lama-Speaks-on-Gay-Sex-He-says-it-s - wrong-2836591.php

(31) "Bible Abuse Directed at Homosexuals." The Roman Centurion -. St. John's MCC Community Website, n.d. http://www.stjohnsmcc.org/new/ BibleAbuse/TheCenturion.php

http://www.gaychristian101.com/Gay- Centurion.html

http://wouldjesusdiscriminate.org/ biblical_evidence/gay_couple.html

http:// www.wouldjesusdiscriminate.org/biblical_evidence/ born_gay.html

https://www.biblegateway.com/passage/?search=Matthew+8%3A5-13%2CLuke+7%3A1-10&version=NIV

(32) "Homosexuality and Christianity." - ReligionFacts. N.p., n.d http:// www.religionfacts.com/homosexuality/ christianity.htm

(33) "Hinduism." - ReligionFacts. N.p., n.d. http:// www.religionfacts.com/homosexuality/ hinduism.htm

(34) Sivaya, Satguru. Dancing with Śiva: Hinduism's Contemporary Catechism. India: Himalayan Academy, 1991 http://western-hindu.org/2012/01/12/hinduism-and-homosexuality/

(35) "Islam and Homosexuality." Islam and Homosexuality. http://www.missionislam.com/ knowledge/homosexuality.htm

(36) https://english.alarabiya.net/en/News/middle-east/2013/05/21/ Lawyer-Two-Moroccans-jailed-for-homosexuality-

https://stage.wikiislam.net/wiki/Persecution_of_Homosexuals_(Saudi_Arabia)

(37) "Morocco: Homosexuality Convictions Upheld." Morocco: Homosexuality Convictions Upheld. http://www.hrw.org/news/2014/07/08/ morocco-homosexuality-convictions-upheld

(38) "Homosexuality and Child Sexual Abuse." Family Research Council. http://www.frc.org/ get.cfm?i=IS02E3

(39) Bryner, Jeanna. "Children Raised by Lesbians Do Just Fine, Studies Show." LiveScience. TechMedia Network, 08 Feb. 2010.

(40) "Aussie Kids Thrive with Gay Parents." Washington Blade Gay News Politics LGBT Rights ICal. N.p., n.d. Web. https://www.washingtonblade.com/2013/06/12/gay-health-aussie-kids-thrive-with-gay-parents-lgbt-news/

(41) Whitam, Frederick L. "Pacific Center for Sex and Society - Homosexual Orientation in Twins: A Report on 61 Pairs and Three Triplet Sets." Pacific Center for Sex and Society - Homosexual Orientation in Twins: A Report on 61 Pairs and Three Triplet Sets. http://www.hawaii.edu/PCSS/ biblio/articles/1961to1999/1993-homosexual- orientation-in-twins.html

(42) "New Study Links Homophobia with Homosexual Arousal." New Study Links Homophobia with Homosexual Arousal. http://www.philosophy-religion.org/handouts/ homophobia.htm

(43) Sanders, Joshunda. "Media Portrayal of Black Youth Contributes to Racial Tension." TheGrio. http://thegrio.com/2012/05/29/media-portrayal-of-black-youth-contributes-to-racial-tension/

(44) Team, Nchhstp Media. New HIV Infections in the United States (n.d.). http://thegrio.com/2012/05/29/media-portrayal-of-black-youth-contributes-to-racial-tension/

www.ingramcontent.com/pod-product-compliance
Lightning Source LLC
Chambersburg PA
CBHW050603300426
44112CB00013B/2047